Praise for

Your Personality Kingdom's
Why Can't Everyone Be Like Me?

"This is a terrific book with a great message, a message that is easy to understand and practical to use."

John Skipper, Globe Gazette and author of
Meredith Willson—The Unsinkable Music Man

"I love this book! Entertaining. Hooks our interest right from the start. Educational process begins in the first paragraph. What a delight to read."

Betsy Goetz, University English Professor

It's like *Who Moved My Cheese,* meets
Myers-Briggs, meets *Harry Potter!*

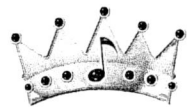

"Once upon a time...

In a land far, far away, there lived the four spirits of personality styles. Like a song of four-part harmony, each one was needed. They each possessed certain character traits that the others lacked. They each brought to the kingdom their unique talents, complementing the others' deficiencies.

...It was therefore decided that the royal subjects of The Personality Kingdom would use a unique method to name their citizens. Everyone observed the behavior of the newcomer, watched how fast they walked, where they got their energy, how they made a decision, what their gestures were, and so on. And because this was a musical land, they thought it would be fun and easy to pose a question for the naming ceremony:

How do you dance through life?

So it came about that the four spirits of personality styles—The Royal Quartet—all had names that represented a type of dance."

... from Chapter Two – The Legend

Why can't everyone be like me?

Because, like a song of four-part harmony, each Personality Kingdom is needed.

Do you waltz through life? Are you peaceful, low-key, and easy-going?
Then you are from the kingdom of…

Waltz the Warm-Hearted
"Relax—Have a Nice Day"

or

Do you salsa through life? Are you a born dynamic, fast-paced leader?
Then you are from the kingdom of…

Salsa the Supreme
"Achieve Great Things—Do it Now!"

or

Do you tango through life? Are you more serious, detailed, and precise?
Then you are from the kingdom of…

Tango the Thinker
"Have Order—Strive for Perfection"

or

Do you swing through life? Are you full of energy, charisma, and fun?
Then you are from the kingdom of…

Swing the Star!
"Have Fun!"

Or maybe you are a combination. How do you dance through life? It's not what kind of music you like. Just imagine your personality becoming a dance! (These characters are meant to represent a personality style, regardless of age, race, gender or nationality.)

Celesta Pines Press
Box 512
Mason City, Iowa 50402
641.423.2123 www.harmony4.net
e-mail: CelestaPines@msn.com
or Harmony4you@hotmail.com

Copyright © 2003 by Kimberly West
All rights reserved. This book, or parts thereof, may not
be reproduced in any form without permission.
Editing support by Susan Kendrick
Cover Design by Lightbourne

Library of Congress Cataloging-in-Publication Data

West, Kimberly
Why Can't Everyone Be Like Me? A magical way to success & harmony
by understanding the four personality styles / Kimberly West
p. cm.

ISBN 0-9742514-0-2   Pre-Pub. Manual Edition (paperback)
1. Personality Types (Psychology) 2. Temperament 3. Diversity I. Title.

155.2'3—dc21   2003-107502
                                CIP

A hardback edition (ISBN 0-9742514-1-0) will be available for special quantity
discounts to use as premiums or for special programs, including corporate training.
For details contact Celesta Pines Special Markets,
Box 512, Mason City, IA 50402, or call 641.423.2123.

Printed in the United States of America
10 9 8 7 6 5 4 3 2

"…Our life is composed, like the harmony of the world, of contrary things, also of different tones, sweet and harsh, sharp and flat, soft and loud… We must learn to embrace what we cannot avoid…"

MICHEL DE MONTAIGNE
(1533-1592)

harmony, n. …justified adaptation of parts to one another, so as to form a connected whole…

WEBSTER'S DICTIONARY

Your Personality Kingdom™
Like four part harmony, each personality is needed.

*...A sweet chorus rang up from the tinseled hue,
"We believe in you, all of us, all of us do!
Don't let your music hide so inside
for your future is bright and yours to decide!"*

FROM THE POEM, THE GIFT—KIMBERLY WEST

I dedicate this book to
the composer of all the music of life.
I hope you are pleased with my song.

And to my family.
Without them, victory would be joyless.

Your Personality Kingdom's
Why Can't Everyone Be Like Me?

INTRODUCTION **13**
THE MAKING OF THE LEGEND **17**

PART ONE ♪ MODERN PROBLEMS
1. Lunch at MicroSurf, Cedar Springs, Iowa **23**

PART TWO ♪ THE LEGEND
"Why Can't Everyone Be Like Me?" **29**
2. The Four Personality Styles: The Royal Quartet **31**
3. Shared Personality Traits **51**
4. The Buddies–Meeting Important Social Needs **65**
5. The Enchantment by Discord the Intolerant **71**
6. In a Perfect World, Everyone Is Just Like Me! **75**
7. The Four Keys to The Harmony Principle **81**
8. The Magic Box **97**

PART THREE ♪ BENEFITS OF THE HARMONY PRINCIPLE
9. Solutions to Modern Problems **103**
10. Success and the Magic Map **121**
11. More is revealed **125**

PART FOUR ♪ AUTHOR'S NOTE & REFERENCE CHARTS
Author's Note **131**

Self-Scoring Personality Test 133

At-a-glance—The Four Personality Kingdoms **137**
Words That Are *Music To My Ears* **157**
Easy Ways to Identify Personality Style Chart **158**
Decisions, Conflict, Problem-Solving Chart **159**
Personality Styles Comparison Chart **160**

Postscript — Contact us **161**
Order Form **163**
About the Author **169**

ACKNOWLEDGMENTS

"Be wealthy in your friends."
WILLIAM SHAKESPEARE

I have been blessed with many friends over the years, and I want to thank several key people that were instrumental in making *Why Can't Everyone Be Like Me?* a reality.

Borden Plunkett, college communications instructor, for being the first person, outside my family, to enthusiastically believe in my vision and me.

Betsy Goetz, university college professor, for her generous spirit and keen editing eyes. And to her mother, thanks! Also to Sheila Bash of the Mason City Library.

Jay Torrey and Steve Faulkner from the Iowa Department of Vocational Rehabilitation for their belief in me, and the EWD financial support, made my dream a reality. Also thanks to all the staff at First State Bank in Nora Springs.

Rich Peterson, from the Iowa Small Business Development Center, for his fun, positive support. And John Skipper, who gave me valuable feedback.

Thanks to Jennifer Handeland from Buena Vista University, David Lee and others who read the early editions of the manuscript. Their input was invaluable.

Deb and Dwight Boisen who gave sanctuary to a stranger.

Ed Jenkins for his untiring help, and for giving me my first computer.

Scott Bell, from the Waltz Kingdom, who named *Please* and *Thank-You*.

Matthew and Nicole Peterson who first created a map of my vision.

Sam Horn, Susan Kendrick and Shannon Bodie for giving the book the polished touches that make it special. Their determination for excellence was a prize.

Thanks to Ken Wind for his detailed drawings of the royal houses and map of my imaginary kingdom, a truly gracious and talented Waltz/Tango.

My Aunt Linda for her generosity and editing expertise.

And to my "other families," The Borcherdings and The Duesenbergs, for their love, support and encouragement. And a special thanks to Amanda for helping with the test.

My family, who are my best friends, for years of deep talks from Tango's Palace and many years of fun from Swing's Tree House! Kathy, Russ, Karen, and Kelly, my best memories are laughing with you so hard my sides still hurt! A special thanks to Kathy for her incredible enthusiasm and big vision for this project.

For my dad, Jerry, who always dreamed big and passed on his hopes to me.

And finally, to my mother, Jeanette, who deserves the gold, no—the platinum medal, for listening to my non-stop ideas with the interest only a mother can give. But most importantly, thanks for telling me to dream big!

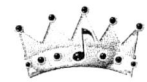

Your Personality Kingdom's

Why Can't Everyone Be Like Me?

KIMBERLY WEST

SPECIAL PRE-PUBLICATION, MANUAL EDITION – SEE PAGE 161

(STANDARD 5 ½ X 8 ½ HARDBACK EDITION TO FOLLOW)

INTRODUCTION

"Simplicity is the key-note in any endeavor."

OG MANDINO—THE GREATEST SECRET IN THE WORLD

This fun, easy book introduces you to the world of personality styles. It will enlighten you to the concept that we are not all the same, and that's a good thing! It will give you a brief understanding of exactly what the four personality styles are and also a very unique and fun way to help you remember them. It will show you that no matter how hard you try to change someone's natural tendencies, it won't work. Nor is there any reason to change them, because all four personality styles are needed to create a world full of perfect harmony.

Learning this important concept is not meant to label people or pigeonhole them, but rather to help understand ourselves and others. This enchanting story will give you a special vocabulary to take back with you to use in the workplace, at home, or at school. Most importantly it will answer the question, "Why can't everyone be like me?"

What is a personality style? It is a set of predictable behaviors or actions that are consistent throughout a person's life. This concept of human temperaments has been documented in dozens of books. In fact, 2,500 yeas ago, Hippocrates devised a method to categorize groups of people by their body chemistry.

Basically there are four types of personality styles, divided into extrovert or introvert and thinking or feeling approaches to life. Some researchers have stated that there are eight types, or nine, or sixteen. Some even contend that there must be thirty-two! Most agree with Hippocrates that there are basically four major temperaments.

Some people are a combination of styles, and some people do change a bit over their lifetime. There is also some debate as to whether these traits are inborn or acquired over time. While upbringing and environment certainly play a part in your personality development, most agree that the basic structure of human temperaments is inherited. That is why twins can be raised in the same environment, go to the same school, have the same parents, and turn out with opposite personality styles!

This book is written as a parable. Instead of telling you about each personality style by listing specific traits, I thought it would be fun—and easier to remember—if I just told you a story using characters that represent each of the four styles.

Why Can't Everyone Be Like Me?

As you read this book, you will find a quartet of sections. In the first section, *Modern Problems,* four co-workers, each with a distinct personality style, talk about their communication problems at work and in their personal lives. You will start learning about each personality style right from the first paragraph!

The second section is the parable, *The Legend of Why Can't Everyone Be Like Me?* This is the heart of the book. A mysterious woman tells the four co-workers an enchanting story to give them answers to their communication problems. She introduces them to a magical kingdom where the spirits of personality styles live. With a smile, the four friends realize that these personalities seem a lot like each one of them!

The four friends learn how these personalities brought their unique talents and skills to the land and how they lived together in perfect harmony until a stranger led them astray. How they find their way back is the key to **The Harmony Principle.**

In the third section, our modern co-workers discuss who they could relate to in the story, and how they can use **The Harmony Principle** in their work and in their lives. And, they find an unexpected surprise! The fourth section is a summary of the four personality styles and charts for easy reference. A quick personality test completes this section.

After reading and using this book, you will be able to identify the four basic personality styles, strengths, and weaknesses. You will know what your Personality Kingdom is—how you dance through life! You will find out where you get your energy, how you make a decision, how you relate to people, and how you like to solve problems. And finally, you will be able to appreciate the special person you are and recognize that we need all four styles in the world to create a place of perfect harmony.

You will be able to apply these simple, yet far-reaching principles, to your work and your personal life. You will experience a clearer direction of what career is best for you. If you practice **The Harmony Principle,** your life will be filled with more peace, and less stress. You will find yourself amused, not frustrated, when you recognize certain personalities. Your relationships will become richer and more harmonious. You will be able to get along with just about anyone!

Some readers of this book's early manuscript chose to stop at the end of The Legend, without reading further, anxious to apply what they had learned. Others, depending on their personality style, enjoyed reading the whole text because it showed them examples of how to apply The Legend to their own lives—and because they wanted to know how the story ended! As you enjoy reading this engaging story, you will hardly notice that you are learning all about the strengths and weaknesses of each personality style.

However you read this book, I know that each time you read *Why Can't Everyone Be Like Me?* you will find something unique and valuable in it. The more you read it, the more meaning you will find. You may read it quickly and be able to appreciate the basic message. You may want to go back and use it as a reference guide, as it is rich in information. I know you will continue to enjoy this engaging story for years to come and remember to sing your special part to make a world full of perfect harmony!

While there are many success principles that shape your destiny in business and in your personal life, there is no other single factor that affects every aspect of your life more than your personality style.

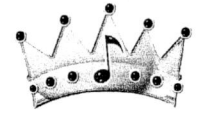

Your Personality Kingdom
Like four part harmony, each personality is needed.

The Making of
The Legend

"The universe is full of magical things

patiently waiting for our wits to grow sharper."

EDEN PHILLPOTTS

Are you curious how this unique book came to be?

Like many people, I love to analyze and understand human behavior. I have been fascinated with understanding the concept of different personality styles for years, and I have read dozens of books on the subject.

I have also read many other self-help and business books over the years. I have attended many business and relationship presentations—and came to an important conclusion: while there are many success principles that shape your destiny in business and in your personal life, there is no other single factor that affects more aspects of your life than your personality style.

Your inborn temperament can affect every major decision you make. It determines where you get your energy, how you go about making a decision, how you solve problems, how you like to organize—or not organize—your life, what kind of person you are attracted to, and so on. Understanding the different personality styles can make a profound impact in your life.

My own life was greatly changed by applying these principles to my business and personal life. When I first learned about the four personality styles, I was working for a small business owner in her office. As a marketing consultant, I enjoyed the creative aspect of the job. The problem was that it was a one-person office—me. I couldn't understand why I felt so drained every day. I wasn't getting any energy. Having survived a near-fatal car accident several years before left me with chronic fatigue syndrome. Therefore, energy became a very important issue to me. Because my boss was so flexible in my scheduling, I stayed.

Then, I learned about the concept of different personality styles. When I realized I needed to interact with other people—that it wouldn't drain me of energy, but actually energize me—I understood that I needed to make a drastic change in my life. I also knew I loved to help people understand the concept of different personality styles. I thought if I could come up with a special presentation on this topic, I could give it my short burst of energy, then have time to recuperate. At the same time, I had a desire to bring the joys of music and couple dancing—ballroom, Latin, and swing dancing—to the general public. I wasn't sure how to promote these two diverse interests, I just knew that I had a passion for both.

With a background in teaching, counseling, and speaking, I became eager to share these personality principles with as many people as possible. I started giving presentations on this subject in a traditional manner. Then, I moved to a place where I was surrounded by music!

It wasn't until I spent time in my family's hometown of Mason City, Iowa—the real "River City" from The Music Man; lived within a few miles of the famed Surf Ballroom—Buddy Holly's last concert; and worked next to a museum with the puppets from The Sound of Music; that I put them all together—music, dance, and the concept of personality styles.

The first part of designing a live presentation was a joy. Instead of asking people what their "behavior temperament" was, or their "cognitive learning style," I wanted to create a *fun* way to refer to the different styles. This led me to pose a question, "How do you dance through life?"

I used costumed ballroom dancers as live visual aids to show the participants what their personality style looked like and sounded like! "Do you waltz through life?" I would ask the audience. "Are you calm and flowing? Or, do you salsa through life with a bold and dynamic style? Do you tango through life with precise, planned movements, or do you swing through life, full of energy and fun?" It wasn't a question of what *kind of music* a person liked, but of imagining their personality *becoming* a dance and type of music.

The crowds loved it! It was so much fun to watch the dynamic dancers show, not tell, each personality's traits. Many people told me how valuable learning these insights had been to them. One woman said that she came to truly value her husband's opposite personality style because it brought balance to her life. Another shy attendee said he wished that he had heard this seminar before he went to nursing school, as he eventually ended up quietly helping people one-on-one as a therapist.

These reactions did not surprise me. I knew how valuable understanding this important concept was. I also knew that when the mind is fully engaged, especially with music, and moving visual aids, it is easier to remember and recall new ideas. What did surprise me was how many people had never heard of this concept before.

Why Can't Everyone Be Like Me?

The demand for videos and audiotapes was understandable. Many people went home or back to their offices and excitedly shared the concept with friends and family. But many people also wanted a book. Now, I was faced with a special challenge. How could I capture the essence of a concept that relied on hearing and seeing movement, in the printed word?

I then re-read and examined the existing books on the subject. Most of them contained very valuable information. But some books were so long and complicated that many readers would get confused and give up. In fact, usually just one personality style enjoys a lot of detail, so by the author's own analysis, that left the majority of people not hearing this important message!

I was determined to come up with a totally fresh, groundbreaking approach that would suit most people. I wanted the book to be fun, easy, to-the-point, yet filled with enough interesting detail so as to not bore anyone either. In other words, why not write the book to the specific types of personality styles that I would be teaching about?

Seeking inspiration, the spirits of personality styles seemed to whisper to me: "Why not create an enchanted land with real characters that personify each behavior style?" I loved it!

So, I kept the dance theme placing each personality character on a musical river of energy. Depending on where they lived on The Crescendo River determined his or her personality style. Wow! An abstract concept came to life!

Being a lover of enchanted stories and classic business books, I let my imagination run free! Also inspired by current bestsellers, I knew that a parable format had been proven as a fast and easy way for readers to learn. So instead of *telling* you traits from each personality style in a traditional "how-to" format, I thought I would *show* you them instead! And that is the birth of *The Legend of Why Can't Everyone Be Like Me?*

I loved writing this book. I'm sure you will love reading it. How could you not? I wrote it with you in mind!

Part One

Modern Problems

Cedar Springs, Iowa

Chapter One

Lunch at MicroSurf Internet Company

Cedar Springs, Iowa

Modern Characters at MicroSurf Internet Company
  Wendy would waltz through life, peaceful and easy-going.
  Thomas would tango through life with precise and analytical thoughts.
  Suzi would swing through life, full of fun and energy.
  Sergio would salsa through life with a bold and dynamic style.

"Celesta Pines Manor... even the name sounds intriguing. Wendy, are you going there tomorrow to The Victory Ball fund-raiser?" asks Thomas, picking a piece of wilted lettuce off the cafeteria tuna-on-rye. Even though Thomas was just a college intern, starting out in the mailroom, he is impeccably groomed. He walks in wearing his usual clean, white polo shirt and pressed black jeans. Even, every short, raven-colored hair knows its place.

"Oh, yes," Wendy says, slowly pouring dressing on her salad. "My husband is in Boston on a business trip, so Suzi and I are going together. And I love to look at all those costumes and see so many nice people. Besides, I'm on the decorating committee."

Why Can't Everyone Be Like Me?

Four friends sit together at a table in the large office lunchroom. The sunny, carpeted room is modern in design with success posters on the walls to motivate the employees: "Good Managers in One Minute," "Enjoy Change," and "Have Fun!" greet them at the door. The employees are a fun lot, but hardworking, too. Yes, MicroSurf is a state-of-the-art Internet Company. Management cared about the personal and business lives of their most valuable asset—their employees. They always brought in the best speakers to their small hamlet to teach the latest success principles. Learning about change, excellent customer service, and having fun while working made everything run smoothly.

It's Friday at 11:45 a.m., and the place is buzzing with talk of weekend plans.

"Oh yeah, I forgot," Thomas says. "You are always helping someone! Well, I don't know what I'm supposed to wear. This is the first time I've been invited and I want to wear the proper costume. Maybe I could go as Leonardo da Vinci. That would be impressive."

At this point, Suzi, a bubbly, colorfully dressed accountant, breezes in and plops down next to Thomas. "Oh, how fun, Tommy! You could paint a Mona Lisa on your polo shirt. Ha! Ha!" She playfully takes his butter knife and pretends to paint the famous smile on Thomas's shirt. He winces as she invades his space.

"Very funny, Suzi," Thomas says. "Just don't call me Tommy. Anyway, I'm serious. The invitation says black-tie or costume required. I want to make sure I don't make a fool of myself and not get invited next year. My invitation got delayed in the mail; otherwise, I would have had plenty of time to plan for it."

"All right," Suzi says. "The ballroom is so elegant at Celesta Pines that most people do have fun dressing up as famous people from bygone eras. I think da Vinci would be wonderful. With your artistic sense, you would make a great…"

Sergio, a tall, attractive sales executive, finally joins the conversation. "Well I hate to interrupt you, Suzi, but where is Thomas going to get a da Vinci costume in one day? The bottom line is that we should get back to business and finish up today's work, or nobody is going anywhere."

Sergio stands up briskly and tells the others where to put the lunch trays as if they didn't know. Flashing a set of dazzling white teeth he continues, "You know I'd love to talk about The Victory Ball, so long as we get those month-end reports done by three o'clock. Thomas, tomorrow I'll pick you up at six. It will work out because my wife insists I still go while she baby-sits our new grandchild. And Thomas, if you do go as da Vinci, maybe I'll go as Michelangelo and we could have a paint off!"

Laughing, they all get up and go back to work. They are an unusual quartet of friends. Normally they wouldn't have become so close, but circumstances had flung them together. When MicroSurf was in its infancy, the company recruited the best people for the new Midwest technology center in Iowa: "Silicorn Valley" as it was affectionately known. They all came from different parts of the country and went through orientation together. Since they didn't know anyone in the quaint river city of Cedar Springs, Iowa, they counted on each other for professional and social support.

THE VICTORY MASQUERADE BALL AT

CELESTA PINES MANOR

SOME ENCHANTED EVENING....

A few people linger in the elegant ballroom during the close of festivities while a light snow begins to fall outside. Celesta Pines Manor is decorated like King Arthur's Court. Golden balloons frame the polished dance floor. Shimmering fabrics of purple and emerald drape the tall windows that fill three sides of the ballroom in the expansive, Tudor-style mansion. The aroma of Irish Crème coffee still lingers in the air while Her Majesty's Orchestra winds down with the last few songs of the evening: a sparkling swing, a supreme salsa, a perfect tango and a heart-warming waltz.

Wendy, Thomas, Suzi, and Sergio are engrossed in conversation with each other. They all have on historic costumes. Sergio is dressed as Julius Caesar. Wendy gracefully moves as Florence Nightingale. Thomas is wearing an elegant, black tuxedo with tails. And Suzi is radiant, if not a little chilly, as Lady Godiva!

Suzi can easily be heard above the music. "Only one guy didn't ask me to dance because he said I was 'too beautiful'—I think I just intimidated him," she pouts. But then she laughs, stretches out her arms, and says in a loud, childlike voice, "Everybody else loved me!"

Thomas smiles at Suzi, she was just so adorable at times. He then looks across the confetti-strewn ballroom. Outside the snow is falling, there is a full moon tonight, and the stars are out. He then spots the lady of the Manor, and event benefactor, Briana Taylor walking toward their group. She is a tall, elegant woman dressed in a queen Guinevere costume with a magnificent, jeweled crown.

"Well, I don't know about all that, Suzi," Thomas says, turning to his hostess. "I know *I* had a most wonderful time, thanks to you, Miss Taylor."

Why Can't Everyone Be Like Me?

"Oh, call me Great Aunt Nana. Everybody else does. And, you are so welcome, Thomas. I'm glad you enjoyed yourself. I loved your costume. It was perfect! And I loved your dry sense of humor when you pulled out that hand-carved paintbrush and announced, 'I need to find my Mona Lisa.' We all thought it very clever!"

Sergio interjects, "Cut to the chase, Thomas. You were nervous, weren't you?"

"Well, yes," Thomas says in a shy voice. "I was trying to not look nervous in front of that beautiful girl. How was I to know there would be someone named Mona Lisa here at the ball tonight? And someone I've been trying to meet at school for months."

Suzi chimes in, "I think she really liked you, Thomas. Although it was hard to tell from her smile." They all laugh. Suzi is roaring the loudest! She loves to laugh at any joke, especially one she comes up with herself.

Great Aunt Nana has been listening to them while looking out the windows. "Oh, my! This snowstorm has suddenly taken a nasty turn for the worst. Celesta Pines is set so far back from the road, you will never be able to get out tonight. You will all just have to spend the night here. I will make the necessary arrangements. Please come with me to the east-wing sitting room, and I'll have my sister bring in some of her freshly baked chocolate chip cookies! We can all have a good chat before you retire for the night."

After a few phone calls home, the four friends enter a cozy sitting room with a crackling fire in the hearth. Hot chocolate is served in delicate hand-carved pine goblets. Overstuffed sofas and chairs are arranged in front of the fire, as scented candles glow on top of a wardrobe. Everybody but Thomas knows Great Aunt Nana, so they feel comfortable at her estate. The four friends are busy talking away as they lounge comfortably.

After a while, Great Aunt Nana joins them. "Don't let me interrupt your conversation," she says. "It sounds like you are all intense about one thing or another! What's it all about?"

WHO MOVED MY HARMONY?

Wendy apologizes saying, "Sorry for the loud voices. We were just discussing some problems we are having. I told them we really should be more positive, especially after such a wonderful party."

Just then, Suzi wails, "I still want to know what I'm doing that keeps pushing men away. I'll be an old maid if I don't get married pretty soon."

Why Can't Everyone Be Like Me?

Sergio is like a father to Suzi and wants to help her. "Look, Suzi, you are just too loud sometimes. You talk too much and that scares men away. The fact that you are funny, charming, and beautiful may be a way to attract men, but not to keep them." This line sounds hauntingly familiar to Suzi, like one from her mother's favorite movie. When her mother married an O'Hara there was no doubt that her pretty, bubbly daughter would be named Suzi Scarlett O'Hara!

Briana Taylor quietly sits back in her favorite chair and sips her hot chocolate while the four friends all start talking at once, going on about their problems. This was a continuation of an ongoing discussion they frequently had.

Thomas starts in, saying, "I don't know what career to go into. My father insists that I enter the Marines like him and my grandfather before him, but I want to be an artist. I don't know how to make him understand me."

Wendy moans, "My husband is so controlling! I love him, but he is wearing me out. Of course, I've never told him this; I don't want to hurt his feelings. But he is just like my boss in production."

Then Sergio says sadly, "My teenage son is so shy, I am really concerned about his future job prospects. I keep trying to make him more outgoing, but nothing is working. He doesn't appreciate my efforts to help him. And secretly, I think he really hates me."

Finally, Great Aunt Nana breaks in, "OK, why don't we take it one at a time. I can't understand anybody. Actually, I think I have heard enough of each problem to see that you are all suffering from the same misconception."

They all stop and look at her quizzically.

"It seems that many of your problems stem from the fact that you don't understand the concept of different personality styles. It is a common misconception that people think everyone is like them. They aren't. And that's a good thing. We are all made in a special way. No one person is exactly like another. Yet it seems that nature made us into certain, distinct groups, with predictable personality traits. Most people have some traits from each of the four styles. Some people are a combination, but even then, many people feel at home in one predominate style.

"Basically there are four personality styles, with no one type being the best. In fact, it takes all four styles working together to make the world run smoothly. And like a song of four-part harmony, each personality style is needed to create a beautiful, harmonious song of life. Everywhere in nature, you see all kinds of variety.

If everybody was the same, it would be like a garden with only one kind of flower, or a forest with only one kind of tree."

Great Aunt Nana stops and looks at each of them with a knowing smile. "Maybe an ancient legend I know might help you understand this puzzling human condition," she says. The four friends wonder if The Legend is a secret to her famous success. They had heard bits and pieces of stories about how she overcame many obstacles to become so successful financially and in her wealth of friends and acquaintances.

Great Aunt Nana pulls out a huge, old, leather-bound book from her library and a little wooden chest with leather straps that holds an ancient scroll. The heavy book creaks open and Great Aunt Nana reads aloud to them amid the sound of the crackling fire and the snowstorm now blustering outside.

Part Two

The Legend

"Why Can't Everyone Be Like Me?"

Chapter Two

The Legend

"Why Can't Everyone Be Like Me?"

The Four Personality Styles: The Royal Quartet

This is the story Great Aunt Nana told…

Introduction to The Legend

Once upon a time, in a land far, far away, there lived the four spirits of personality styles. Each one lived in their own kingdom and possessed certain character traits that the others lacked. They each brought their unique talents to the land, complementing the others' deficiencies. Where one was shy, the other was outgoing. Where one was disorganized, the other brought order. Where one was industrious, the other brought fun. Where one was results-focused, the other concentrated on relationships. All four kingdoms lived side-by-side in perfect harmony.

The four spirits of personality styles were actually two sets of twins that lived on *The Crescendo River*. One set of twins was from the Family of Introvert. The other set was from the Family of Extrovert. The twins loved living by this musical river of energy. They all had beautiful singing voices, and much like the way they lived their lives, their velvety voices blended together in perfect harmony to the delight of lords, ladies, and common folk alike.

The two sets of twins were of royal descent and were the most sought-after singing quartet in the land. Therefore the four spirits of personality styles were best known by their group name. They were called *The Royal Quartet*.

Now mind you, a spirit is neither male nor female, but because I am telling you this story in English, I will use the pronoun *he* to be easily understood. It's rather difficult to describe spirits, so you can visualize them as either gender. And even though they were twins, because of their distinct personality styles, each one was quite unique in appearance.

I will tell you The Legend in sections, first describing each member of The Royal Quartet. You will hear what their particular personality strengths are, and how they received their unique names. Secondly, I will give you more detail and show you what their *shared* personality traits are, and how to meet their social needs. Then, I will share with you *The Legend of Why Can't Everyone Be Like Me?* where you will find out what happens when everyone *is* just like you!

THE CRESCENDO RIVER NAMING CEREMONY

"HOW DO YOU DANCE THROUGH LIFE?"

It was decided long ago that the royal subjects of The Crescendo River would use a unique method to name their citizens. Everyone observed the behavior of the newcomer, watched how fast they walked, where they got their energy, and how they made a decision. The naming committee also watched how the new person interacted with people, what kind of clothes they usually wore, and so on. And because this was a musical land, the committee thought it would be fun and easy to pose a question for the naming ceremony, "How does this person *dance* through life?" Not what kind of music they liked, but trying to see their essence becoming a dance and type of music. So it came about that the four spirits of personality styles—The Royal Quartet—all had names that represented a type of dance.

The Four Personality Styles: The Royal Quartet

Character Strengths

The Royal Quartet

Waltz the Warm-Hearted	*Tango the Thinker*
Swing the Star	*Salsa the Supreme*

"Like four-part harmony, each personality kingdom is needed."

Family of Introvert

Tango the Thinker

Royal Inventor's Palace

"Have Order—Strive for Perfection"

FAMILY OF INTROVERT

TANGO THE THINKER

"Anything worth doing is worth doing right."

ANONYMOUS

One twin from the *Family of Introvert* was christened *Tango the Thinker*. He was named such because he was very precise, serious, and formal—like a tango dance. He walked and spoke with a slow cautiousness.

Tango lived in *The Royal Inventor's Palace*, which had elegant Art Deco architecture with perfectly manicured lawns and gardens that matched Tango's appearance. He also looked very neat, trim, and tidy. Every short raven-colored hair knew its place. Both he and his residence looked just perfect.

Tango was *The Royal Inventor*. In fact, he was working on a strange new contraption that had diodes, transistors, and silicon wafers. Tango called it a "computer"–whatever that was! The townspeople laughed at him and said it would go nowhere, but Tango just adjusted his spectacles and smiled. He was very talented in other ways, too. Consequently, in addition to his soothing singing voice, Tango was an accomplished musician and artist. One season he was commissioned to paint a magnificent fresco mural on the town's sea wall.

He loved to think deep thoughts. Tango would ponder on issues and loved to analyze anything, from machines to people. Tango was able to master complicated problems and enjoyed doing so. Consequently, the naming committee christened him "Tango the Thinker."

Tango had a very dry sense of humor. One time he was told that there was a fire up in the mountains. It was said that the fire was intense. He turned to his friend and blankly asked, "Hmm…I wonder how they got the fire in tents up there?"

The motto for the Kingdom of Tango the Thinker was "Have Order–Strive for Perfection."

There was a special naming plaque that the royal subjects issued to everyone they named. It listed the person's character strengths and why the committee chose that particular name for them. Tango decided to put his plaque up in his royal inventor's studio next to his awards in science, music, and literature. His studio was neat and organized with just a few projects on his drafting table.

THE CRESCENDO RIVER NAMING CEREMONY PLAQUE

CHARACTER STRENGTHS—THE KINGDOM OF

TANGO THE THINKER

The Royal Subjects of The Crescendo River have christened you "Tango the Thinker," because you have displayed these character strengths:

Analytical	Conservative
Cautious	Courteous
Deep emotions	Deep thinker
Detailed	Follows the rules
Dry humor	Frugal, thrifty
Duty, honor bound	Intellectual
Genius prone	Low-energy
Gifted	Neat, organized
High-standards	Patient
Likes charts, graphs	Persistent
Methodical	Private
Planner	Problem-solver
Respectful	Proper
Scheduled	Responsible
Serious	Slow and steady
Structured	Works well alone

Family of Introvert

Waltz the Warm-Hearted

Royal Cottage

"Relax—Have A Nice Day"

FAMILY OF INTROVERT

WALTZ THE WARM-HEARTED

"...each smile can be exchanged for gold and each kind word, spoken from my heart, can build a castle..."

FROM THE SCROLL MARKED VII
OG MANDINO—THE GREATEST SECRET IN THE WORLD

The other twin from the Family of Introvert lived across the river. He was named *Waltz the Warm-Hearted*. He loved living in *The Royal Cottage*; a warm and cozy home with a heart-shaped window and smoke curling up from the brick chimney. He was named Waltz because he was low-key, gracious, and flexible, like a flowing Waltz dance. He walked slowly and calmly usually with a friendly, if not a little shy, smile on his face.

Waltz had a very relaxed appearance. His hair was not combed perfectly like his brother Tango, but was more carefree. He liked to wear comfortable clothes and shoes. Sometimes his clothes looked a little frumpy because it might take too much energy to press them. Waltz enjoyed wearing shoes like loafers because it was easier than trying to lace up shoes or boots.

Waltz determined his worth by how many friends he had. And by his own count, he was wealthy, indeed. He was very personable, with a witty sense of humor. Everyone loved to go to the little cottage up in the peaceful mountains, sit in the comfy chairs, and have Waltz listen to what they had to say. It was amazing, they all said, how Waltz could remember to ask about a certain event that was last talked about. "How was your trip to watch the fall leaves?" He would ask the next time he saw you. And being *The Royal Diplomat* provided Waltz with a steady stream of people from all parts of the kingdom. He was the most gracious host to all who entered his cozy retreat.

The motto for the Kingdom of Waltz the Warm-Hearted was, "Relax—Have a Nice Day."

Waltz decided to put his naming plaque up in his kitchen next to his many pictures of family and friends. As most people who came to visit Waltz gravitated to the warm, casual atmosphere of his kitchen, he quietly liked to look at his plaque and see how he was appreciated.

The Crescendo River Naming Ceremony Plaque

Character Strengths -- The Kingdom of Waltz the Warm-Hearted

The Royal Subjects of The Crescendo River have christened you "Waltz the Warm-Hearted," because you have displayed these character strengths:

Accommodating	Adaptable
Agreeable	Considerate
Amiable	Contented
Cautious	Counseling skills
Compassionate	Easy-going
Diplomatic	Good administrator
Gracious	Informal
Humble	Likable
Loyal friend	Patient
Mediator	Prefers first names
Modest	Respectful
Relaxed	Rise to the occasion
Reserved	Shy
Supportive	Steady and calm
Team-player	Tolerant
Sympathetic	Warm & Friendly

Family of Extrovert

Salsa the Supreme

Royal Castle

"Achieve Great Things—Do It Now!"

FAMILY OF EXTROVERT

SALSA THE SUPREME

"Life is a daring adventure or nothing at all."

HELEN KELLER

One twin from the *Family of Extrovert* was named *Salsa the Supreme*. He was named this because he was like a hot, Latin salsa dancer: dynamic, powerful, and confident. Salsa was practical in appearance. He was tidy, organized, and walked with a direct, steady, usually fast gate. He was results-oriented and was always going somewhere in a hurry. Because he was usually thinking of things he had to accomplish, sometimes Salsa had a furrowed brow. He was a dynamic leader, although he did have a sarcastic sense of humor.

Salsa lived in *The Royal Castle*. This castle was very practical and served many purposes. Salsa even had a water wheel on The Crescendo River that supplied all the energy for the kingdom. Salsa was *The Royal Builder,* always building and accomplishing many things at once. Aside from his energy business, Salsa had at least three home-based businesses attached to his castle. He was very active in the community as well. Salsa was the head of the local merchants and travelers association and he served on the board of the Bank of Gold Talents. He strove to be the best at anything he did, as Salsa loved to be supreme in all his endeavors.

The motto for The Kingdom of Salsa the Supreme was, "Achieve Great Things–Do it Now!" Oh, I almost forgot! Salsa was also the General in charge of all the Royal armies.

Salsa decided to put his naming plaque in his work office, as that was where he spent much of his time. His office was very neat and organized like Tango's studio, except that Salsa had many, many projects in his office. Salsa could work on several big projects at any one time. He could master and oversee a number of situations with ease. He put his naming plaque next to the portrait of himself in his General's uniform. He also had several important awards for all his good deeds and many accomplishments. He was especially proud of the charities he had started to help the youth of the land.

The Crescendo River Naming Ceremony Plaque

Character Strengths -- The Kingdom of Salsa the Supreme

The Royal Subjects of The Crescendo River have christened you "Salsa the Supreme," because you have displayed these character strengths:

Accomplished	Ambitious
Adventurous	Brave
Assumes authority	Causes action
Capable	Daring
Commands attention	Delegates tasks
Confident	Doer
Decisive	Fast-paced
Direct	Independent
Dominate	Leader
Industrious	Outspoken
Productive	Persuasive
Resourceful	Powerful
Results oriented	Practical
Take-charge	Problem solver
Tenacious	Risk-taker
Visionary	Strong-willed

Family of Extrovert

Swing the Star

Royal Tree House

"Have Fun!"

FAMILY OF EXTROVERT

SWING THE STAR

"I will laugh at the world. To enjoy success I must have happiness, and laughter will be the maiden who serves me..."

FROM THE SCROLL MARKED VII
OG MANDINO—THE GREATEST SALESMAN IN THE WORLD

The other twin from the Family of Extrovert lived across the river from Salsa. He was named *Swing the Star*. He was christened this because he was like a big-band swing song: high-energy, lively, and dramatic. Swing looked wide-eyed and happy. He usually had a big smile on his bright face as he briskly walked though the kingdom talking to anyone that happened to be near by. No one was a stranger to Swing. He also liked to wear the most fashionable attire of the time, even if it was a little outrageous. Swing loved the attention it brought him.

Swing lived in *The Royal Tree House*. He loved adventure so he designed his home like a sailing ship! There were many levels to Swing's tree house, with a swing made from a small boat, open party decks, and lots of fun toys and game rooms to play in.

Swing was *The Court Jester* because he always made everyone laugh! In fact, laughter was a big part of Swing's life. He laughed very loudly and did so often. Swing did have a tendency to lose things, though. One time he was frantically rummaging through some boxes. Swing turned to Tango and the rest of the party and asked, "Does anyone know what I'm looking for?"

The motto for The Kingdom of Swing the Star was, "Have Fun!"

Swing decided to put his naming plaque in his game room, as this was his favorite place in the house. He put the plaque next to his many pictures of friends and family where he was the center of attention! And it was a good thing the plaque was on the wall, otherwise Swing might not be able to find it again, as his tree house was usually in varying stages of disorganization, but always fun!

THE CRESCENDO RIVER NAMING CEREMONY PLAQUE

CHARACTER STRENGTHS—THE KINGDOM OF SWING THE STAR

The Royal Subjects of The Crescendo River have christened you "Swing the Star," because you have displayed these character strengths:

Animated	Cute
Bubbly	Delightful
Charming	Dramatic
Entertainer	Enthusiastic
Fast-paced	Exciting
Great socializer	Flexible
Happy	Friendly
Involved	Fun-loving
Lively	Funny
Loves action	Intuitive
Playful	Light-hearted
Relationship focused	Optimistic
Risk-taker	Outgoing
Spontaneous	Persuasive
Stimulating	Popular
Talkative	Sparkling

Note: To learn more details about shared personality traits and the social needs of each style, continue reading the next chapters, three and four. To skip this section, go directly to chapter five and continue on with the story.

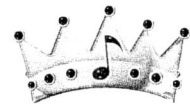

Chapter Three

Shared Personality Traits

Where one lived on the river of energy determined his temperament.

Each twin looked very distinct and had certain personality traits that were easy to predict and delighted the kingdom. However, they did share certain traits with each other, and had things in common. One was obvious—what family they were from, Extroverts or Introverts. The other was less obvious—what side of the river they lived on.

First, we will look at the two Royal Families. The major distinction between these families was where they got their energy. The Family of Introvert received their energy from within. The Family of Extrovert got their energy from others outside themselves.

Shared Personality Traits
Introvert or Extrovert Family

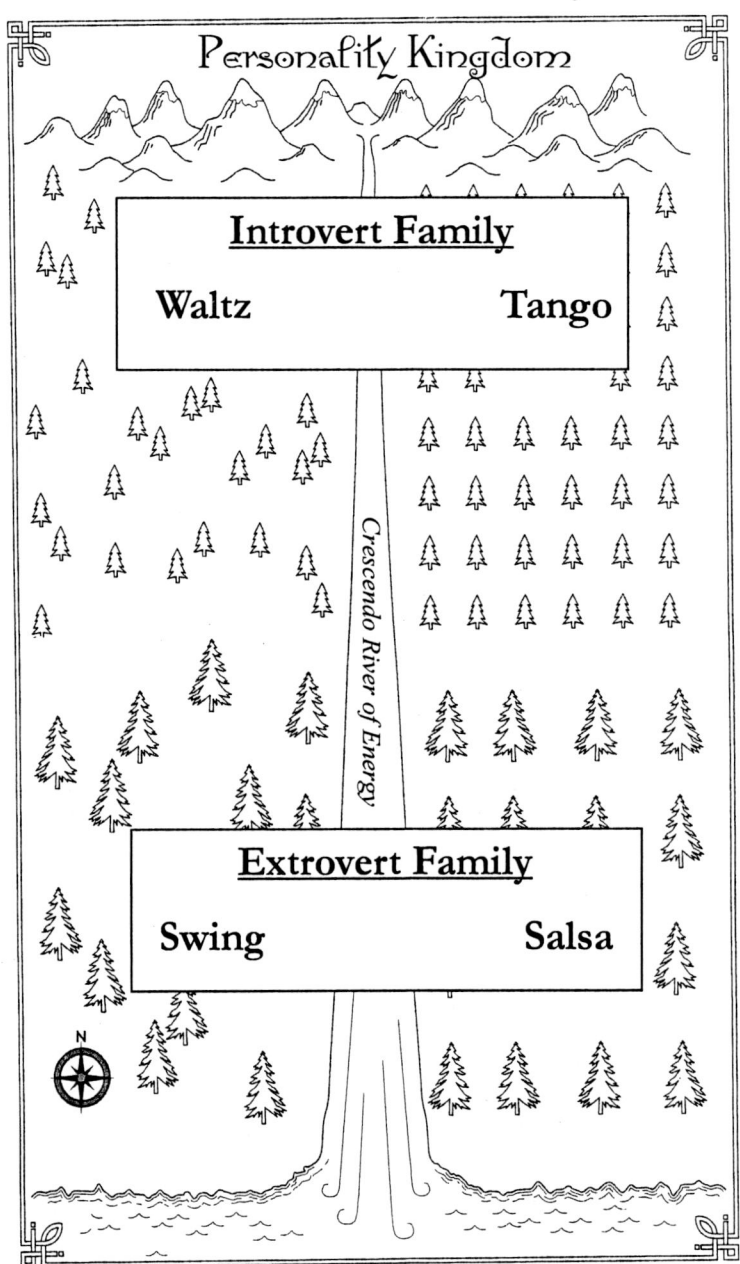

The Family of Introvert—Waltz & Tango

Receiving Energy from Within

One set of twins, Waltz and Tango Introvert, lived at the source of The Crescendo River high up in the *Mountains of Tranquillity* where the river started out as quiet, trickling stream. The fresh smell of wildflowers and evergreens filled this peaceful retreat. The quiet rustling of leaves in the wind was a calming sound to Waltz and Tango.

The Family of Introvert was a rather shy, yet witty lot, slow to get to know, especially around strangers. When Waltz and Tango attended parties, they usually waited for someone else to start a conversation, and spoke to only a few people. Waltz and Tango didn't like change and would rather follow established rules and guidelines.

Introverts get their energy from within and often feel drained if they have to be in crowds of people for any length of time. Waltz and Tango liked to retreat to their respective homes to recharge before venturing out again. When they felt especially drained or stressed, they each went to their special cave in the Mountains of Tranquillity to rest.

Waltz and Tango Introvert were more cautious, less demanding and less confrontational, but they had great inner strength, determination, and a fierce loyalty to their high moral values. An unwavering strong will lurked behind their serene faces.

THE FAMILY OF EXTROVERT—SWING AND SALSA

RECEIVING ENERGY FROM OTHERS

Swing and Salsa, from the *Family of Extrovert,* lived near the south end of The Crescendo River where by now it was a loud, dynamic, full-blown river that emptied out into the *Sea of Adventure.* A bustling town was situated at the mouth of The Crescendo River. From there, tall sailing ships would set out to sea for unknown conquests.

Swing and Salsa Extrovert loved living by the sea because it was constantly in motion. The rhythmic waves were a never-ending comfort to all that lived near the aquamarine waters. Swing and Salsa loved to swim in the salty sea and feel the sand between their toes. The lure of constant motion and energy filled the ocean nights. The aroma of roasting marshmallows, crackling campfires, and melted chocolate had the twins yelling for s'more!

The Family of Extrovert was a fast-paced, direct, out-spoken bunch. Swing and Salsa had high-energy and loved to interact with people. The Extroverts loved to go to parties and usually initiated conversations with many people. Swing and Salsa spoke quickly, with authority and conviction. This family was assertive, competitive and tended to dominate interactions. Swing and Salsa definitely got their energy from interacting with people.

Shared Personality Traits
Introvert or Extrovert Family

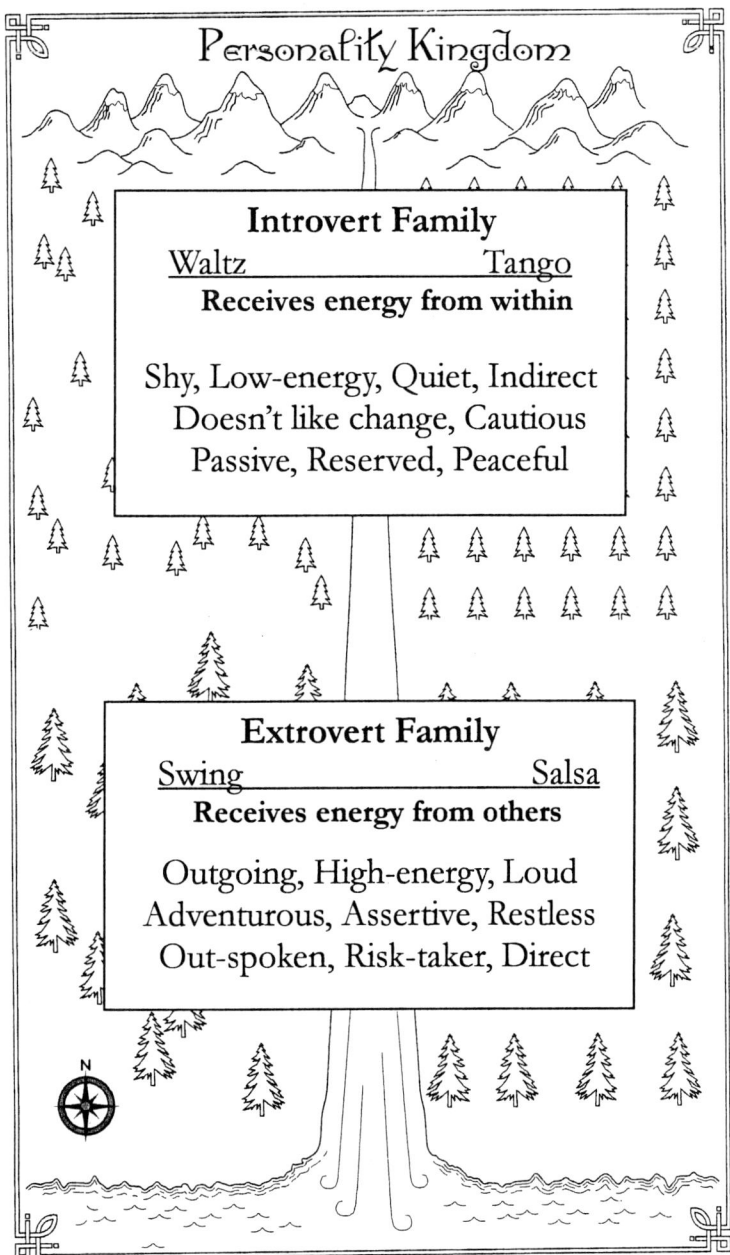

Personality Kingdom

Introvert Family

<u>Waltz</u>　　　　　　　<u>Tango</u>

Receives energy from within

Shy, Low-energy, Quiet, Indirect
Doesn't like change, Cautious
Passive, Reserved, Peaceful

Extrovert Family

<u>Swing</u>　　　　　　　<u>Salsa</u>

Receives energy from others

Outgoing, High-energy, Loud
Adventurous, Assertive, Restless
Out-spoken, Risk-taker, Direct

OTHER SHARED PERSONALITY TRAITS

FEELING OR THINKING APPROACH TO LIFE

WHAT SIDE OF THE RIVER ONE LIVED DETERMINED HIS OUTLOOK ON LIFE.

The second way in which the twins shared certain personality traits depended on which side of the river he lived on. It determined how he liked to structure his time, how formal he was with new people, and if he approached life from a feeling or thinking standpoint.

The side Waltz and Swing lived on was the west riverbank, which was informal and laid-back. Waltz and Swing loved to live there, because it was flexible in planning and scheduling and everyone placed a priority on feelings, people and relationships. This side was called the *West Coast*.

The east riverbank, where Tango and Salsa lived, was more structured and formal. Tango and Salsa liked to plan everything out and had a more guarded approach to people. They focused more on thinking, facts, and results. This side was called the *East Coast*.

Shared Personality Traits
Feeling or Thinking Outlook

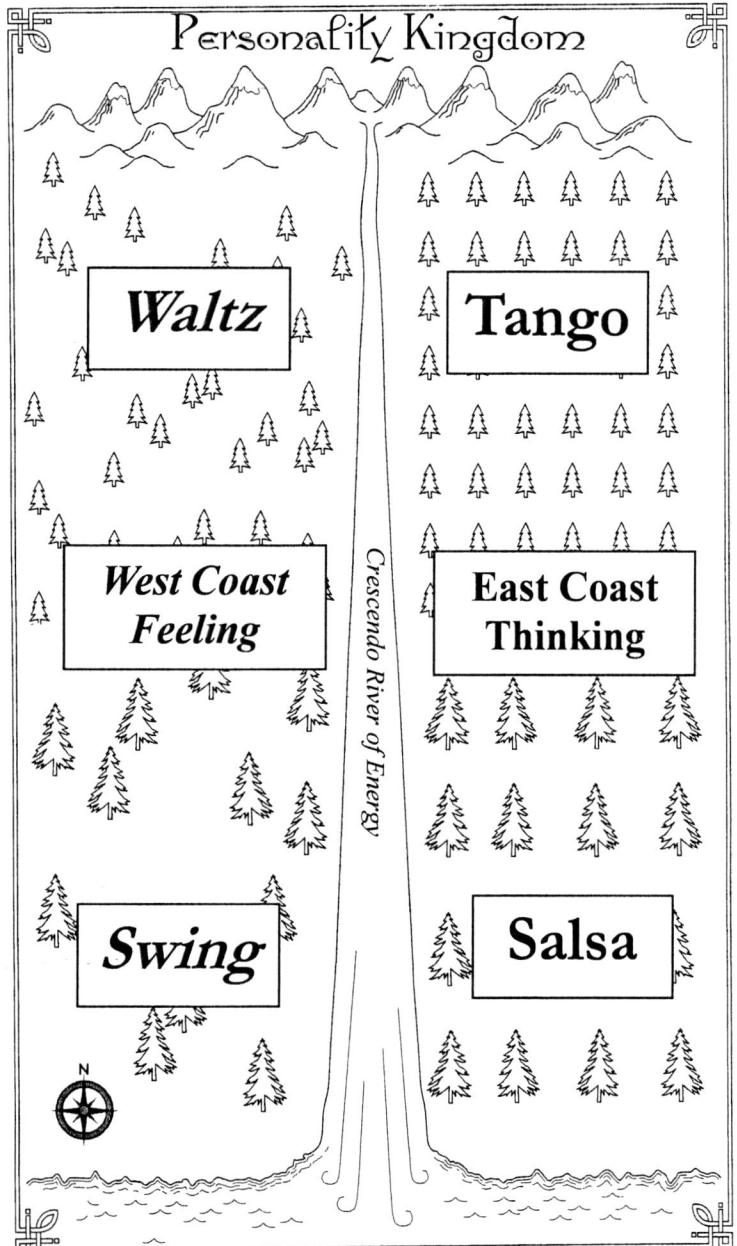

The East Coast – Thinking

Tango & Salsa

More private and serious. Structured by time.

An emphasis on facts and results.

The East Coast had a tall, stone fence that separated the kingdoms of Tango and Salsa. On each side of the fence there were neat, planned rows of flowers, trees, and perfectly trimmed shrubs. Everything was put away, and out of the way, of the neat, angled walkways.

Because planning and scheduling were so important to them, Tango and Salsa had a huge clock, like Big Ben, in the middle of the fence. Because of this formal approach to life, Tango and Salsa liked to live on the East Coast, which tended to be more private and serious. Even though Tango and Salsa came from opposite families—the Family of Introvert and the Family of Extrovert—they did share common ground in that they both lived on the same side of the river. They both approached life from a thinking perspective, making decisions based on facts and results.

Tango and Salsa met only occasionally when they had something to accomplish together. For instance, one time Salsa's waterwheel broke and he came to Tango for engineering plans to build a better one. When they met, they got right down to business, not wanting to waste time on trivial matters.

People who lived on the formal East Coast were private, and didn't readily disclose personal information. Tango and Salsa were more focused on tasks, actions, and facts and stayed on the subject that was being discussed. They liked to work independently, and enjoyed a planned schedule. When in conversation, Tango and Salsa had a limited range of facial expressions, as thoughts, not feelings were more important to them. When they met someone for the first time, Tango and Salsa usually kept their distance physically with a polite and formal handshake.

Like everybody on The Crescendo River, Tango and Salsa had feelings; they just didn't readily express them. Tango especially had very deep feelings, but only a few close people to him were allowed to see them.

Time, and how it was used, was important to both Tango and Salsa, but in different ways.

Salsa's time was very important to him. In fact it was one of his most prized values. He scheduled a lot, and he accomplished a great deal, usually in a short amount of time. Salsa didn't like to have his time wasted by other people loafing around. His time frame was NOW! He used time to accomplish as much as possible as his hands were never idle. Salsa valued quantity.

Time was also important to Tango. But because he was from a different Royal Family, the Family of Introvert, Tango liked to patiently plan his time, carefully plotting out how much was needed to accomplish his goals. Tango used time as a way to weigh matters of today on how they were done correctly in the past. Tango valued quality.

One time, Swing complained that Tango wasn't spontaneous, so Tango scheduled two hours each week to be spontaneous!

Shared Personality Traits
Feeling or Thinking Outlook

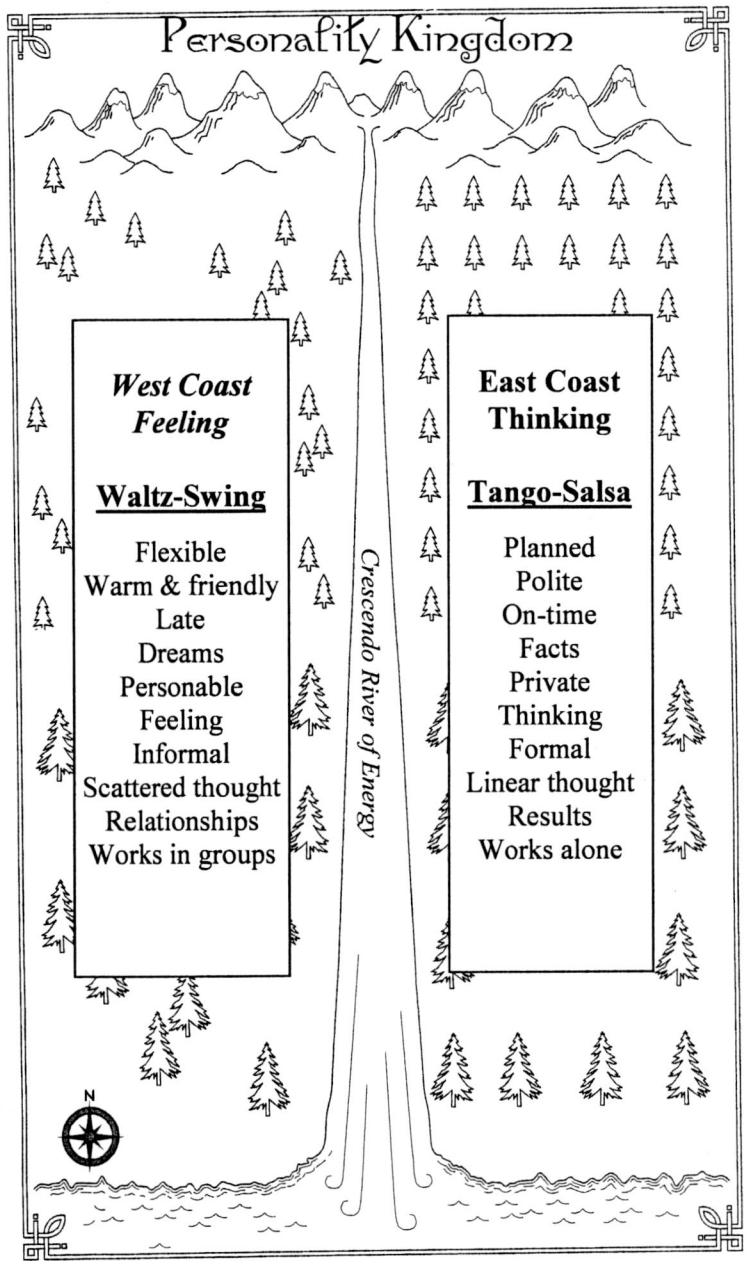

West Coast—Feeling

Waltz & Swing

Flexible planning. Informal.

An emphasis on dreams, visions, relationships.

Waltz and Swing lived on the west riverbank, which was more informal and laid-back. It was known as the *West Coast*. This riverbank had royal palm trees and colorful flowers dotted throughout its land. Normally palm trees wouldn't grow in this region, but because Waltz and Swing were very warm people, the tropical trees thrived.

The landscape was not planned out, but had a flowing, sporadic quality to the curved paths and walkways. It was OK with everybody in the land to let the children sometimes leave their bikes out in front of the houses. Garden tools, wheelbarrows, and other items often stayed where they were last used.

Waltz and Swing had a clock in the middle of their land, too, but it might as well have been broken, because nobody really paid that much attention to it. Waltz and Swing were both flexible, they could "go with the flow." Sometimes a definite time felt confining to them, so they would consequently arrive late sometimes.

Waltz and Swing liked living on this informal side of the river. They cared more about people, feelings, and relationships than staying on a schedule. Waltz and Swing shared common ground by living together on the West Coast, even though they were from different Royal Families. They frequently met at their property border of low, flowering hedges and asked about each other's families and personal life before they ever talked about any business. It just seemed so rude to jump right in and talk of "work."

People who lived in the relaxed atmosphere of the West Coast enjoyed working in groups and wanted to make sure everybody was happy with their decisions. Waltz and Swing were easy to get to know, and openly showed their feelings, even about personal matters. Waltz and Swing had a friendly handshake and were more responsive to dreams, visions, and concepts rather than to facts, figures, and results. They made decisions based on whether it "felt right" to them.

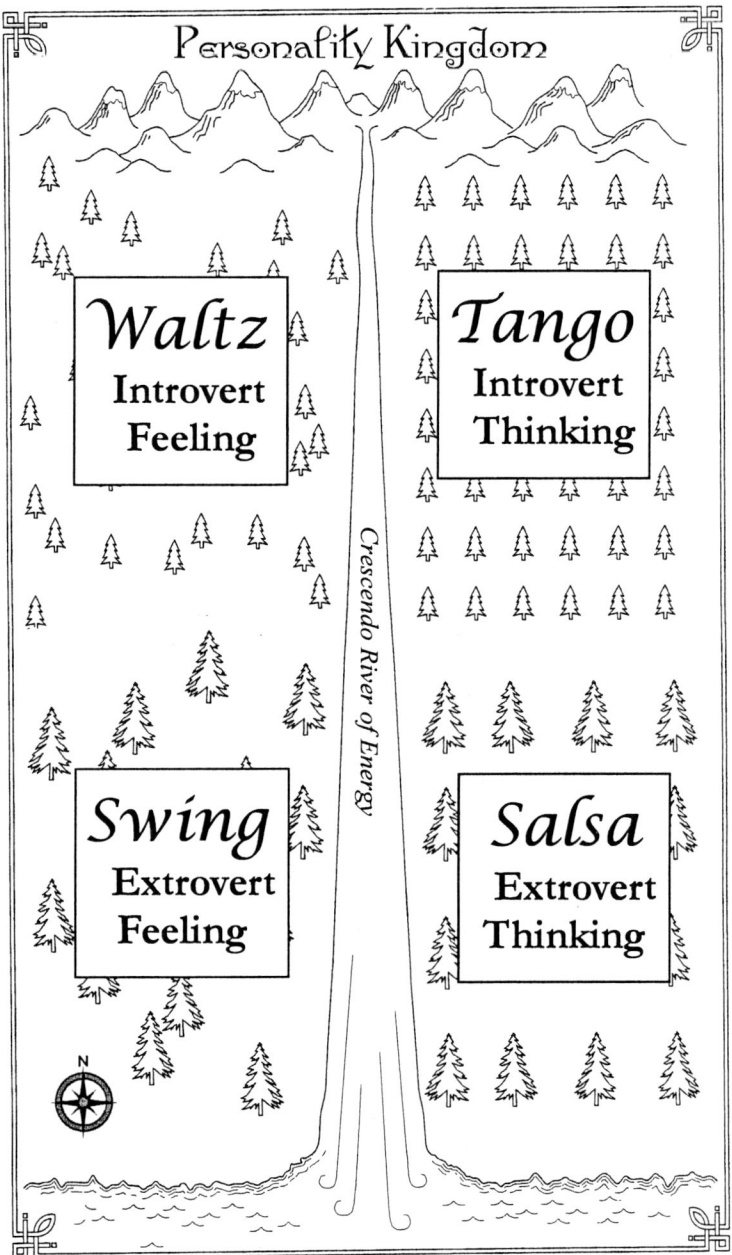

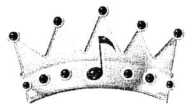

Chapter Four

BUDDIES OF THE ROYAL QUARTET FULFILL IMPORTANT SOCIAL NEEDS.

Each twin had special needs and certain friends that met those needs. When these companions spoke certain words and phrases, the words were so important, they actually became music to each twin's ears. In fact, this expression "music to my ears," came to be used throughout the land.

THE APPRECIATION SISTERS: PLEASE AND THANK-YOU

PLACE HIGH VALUE ON WALTZ

Waltz the Warm-Hearted had the *Appreciation Sisters* as friends named *Please* and *Thank-You*. Before Please wanted to do something, she always *asked* first, never *telling* Waltz what to do. Please was very respectful to Waltz.

Thank-You always told Waltz how much she appreciated him, sending special presents and gifts to show Waltz how much she cared about him. Thank-You also did chores around the house that *showed* him just how special he was. Waltz felt so appreciated when these acts of kindness were given.

OLYMPIA THE JUDGE DECLARES TANGO A "10"

Tango the Thinker had *Olympia the Judge* as a best friend. When Tango showed her a completed project, she always looked at it, thought about it, and judged it a perfect "10."

Once, Tango spent a long time on a project at work. He spent hours inventing a new open spiral slide for Swing's tree house. Tango drew several different plans for this slide. He thought about all angles, and wanted it to be just perfect for Swing's many parties. Once he had an idea in the middle of the night, and got out of bed to draw it on his drafting table before the creative thought left him.

Tango showed Swing all of his hard work. Swing looked at the designs quickly, pointed to one, and said, "I love this one. Have Salsa's team build it for me. Gotta run, thanks!"

Feeling unappreciated, Tango showed his work to Olympia. Giving Tango her full attention, she studied the plans asking questions about how he came up with all those clever ideas. She commented on how precise and detailed the plans were saying it must have taken a long time. She saw the excellent quality of his work and declared it a perfect 10!

FANFARE CELEBRATES SALSA'S ACHIEVEMENTS.

Salsa the Supreme loved to have *Fanfare* as a best friend for she would arrive everywhere ahead of Salsa and announce his coming with a fanfare of trumpet sounds. Ta…Ta, Ta, Ta, Tum! Fanfare would boast, "Announcing the arrival of Salsa the Supreme who accomplishes more in one day than most people do in a week! Winner of many awards, his good deeds are plentiful!" Fanfare valued Salsa's never-ending energy. She made sure that Salsa was in control of most of the projects, because Fanfare knew that control was one of Salsa's most important needs. Fanfare also knew how competent Salsa was and enjoyed trusting in his abilities.

Treating Salsa this way was easy because he really did accomplish an enormous amount of work. Salsa's mind was constantly in motion with ideas shooting off like fireworks on a starry night. He could think about a problem and then with lightening speed come up with, what usually was the correct answer. Salsa did know a lot, and was quite successful at everything he tried.

THE OVATION SISTERS: ENCORE AND APPLAUSE CHEER SWING ON!

Swing the Star loved to have the *Ovation Sisters* as best friends. They were named *Encore* and *Applause*. Whenever Swing told a story, which he loved to do often, Applause would clap loudly, give him a big hug, and say, "You are terrific! That's the funniest story I've ever heard!" Encore would jump to her feet and shout, "Tell it again! Tell it again. You are the best!" Encore and Applause loved Swing and his funny, charming stories. Swing would just swell with pride at hearing such praise. It became music to his ears. He would have done anything for his beloved Ovation Sisters for they gave Swing so much energy.

♪ Words that are "Music To My Ears" ♪
Say them to gain instant rapport with each style

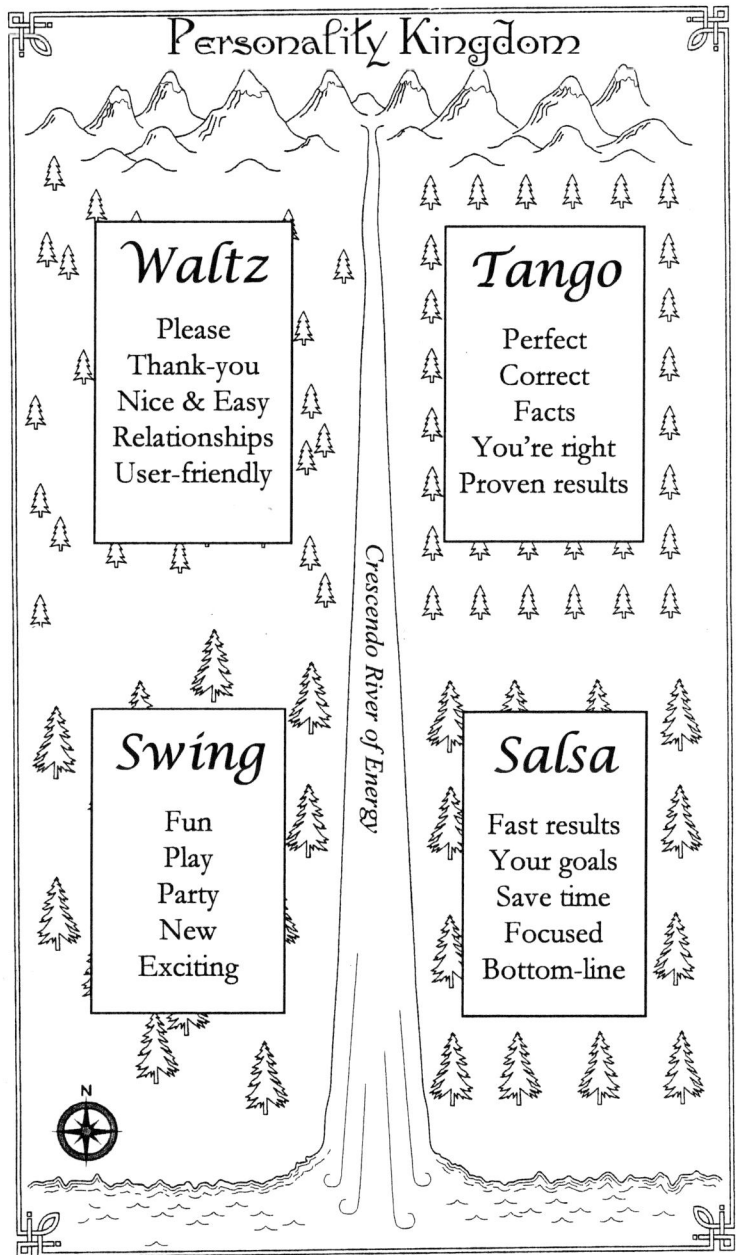

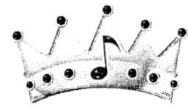

CHAPTER FIVE

DISCORD THE INTOLERANT WREAKS HAVOC ON THE KINGDOM

THE ENCHANTMENT OF THE ROYAL QUARTET

The Royal Quartet was so at peace in their land, that they didn't see a cunning fox, *Discord the Intolerant*, creep into the kingdom one day. Slowly and deviously, Discord put an enchantment on The Royal Quartet, which caused a gradual sense of irritability to come into their lives. They became increasingly intolerant of anyone not like them. Swing couldn't stand it when people were shy and quiet. Salsa started interrupting people if they didn't get right to the point. Tango isolated himself because everybody else was imperfect, and Waltz started keeping a secret score-sheet whenever anyone was boisterous. They didn't notice Discord had become a frequent guest in each of their kingdoms, smiling smugly and making himself at home.

Discord had invaded all aspects of their lives. The enchantment had even affected their singing. Every time they sang a song, the beautiful four-part harmony was gone. It got so bad that eventually they began to sing out of tune. The first time this happened, they all looked at each other and realized something dreadful had occurred. They didn't have a clue as to how it happened, but vowed never to sing together again.

PLANNING OF THE ROYAL FESTIVAL

A ROYAL DISASTER

At this same time, it came about that the kingdom's annual festival was quickly coming upon them. Every year this special time was set aside to celebrate all the unique talents and gifts of the people. Singing, acrobatic, musical and dancing talents were a few of these renowned gifts.

The festivities were set up on the shores of the Sea of Adventure drawing people from far-away corners of the kingdom to witness the astonishing feats of skill.

Each twin naturally took on certain responsibilities for the festival. Salsa was the director in charge of managing the whole affair. Waltz was in charge of assisting the director and was the informal peacekeeper. Swing's job was to be the ringmaster. And, Tango was in charge of all the money that came from various sources. He kept meticulous records of all the gold coins received.

But this year was different. Discord had become fast friends with all the twins, and the enchantment had now run very deep. Nobody thought anything unusual when Discord attended the first planning meeting. In fact, he was welcomed as an honored guest at the beginning of the session. This was Discord's chance. While addressing the twins and the other royal subjects of the land, Discord slyly mentioned that certain duties really should be rotated each year to be fair to everyone. "Why should one person have to do the same thing each year?" he asked. "Wouldn't it be better to change duties every year?" And because of the enchantment, everybody blindly agreed.

It was therefore decided that this year was Tango's turn to be the ringmaster and opening entertainment act. It became Salsa's turn to assist the director and make sure that everybody got along. He was to quietly sit in the audience and take notes for the director. It was Waltz's turn to manage the whole affair, giving assignments to everybody. And finally Swing would be in charge of the money, keeping detailed records of all transactions. He was also in charge of planning and scheduling all the numerous volunteers who helped.

They all went about their duties with the enthusiasm of a new project. But problems quickly arose. Swing kept losing the money and was late all the time. He would feel embarrassed about the lost money and tried to remember how much it was so that he could replace it with his own. Soon, however, his own personal gold cache was dwindling away.

Tango didn't want to get up and be all wide-eyed and enthusiastic in front of a crowd. Whenever Tango tried to rehearse in front of people, he would get drained. He tried to be outgoing, funny, and charming, but instead he just sounded phony.

Salsa wasn't keeping the peace at all—he just kept telling everybody what to do. During rehearsals, he was supposed to quietly make note of performance errors and give them to the director. Instead, he shouted out directions to the performers himself. At one point, the performers got so confused, listening to both their director and Salsa, that they just walked off the set!

For his part, Waltz kept procrastinating in delegating duties. Instead he tried to do everything himself. It just seemed so rude to tell other people what to do. And it was overwhelming to be in charge of the entire affair. Having to lead all the big meetings and make so many decisions was exhausting to Waltz.

When their weekly planning meeting came up, all chaos broke loose. When the other twins found out that Swing kept losing the money, they were furious. And the volunteers hadn't even met because Swing didn't like to stop and plan anything. Tango couldn't understand how anybody could mess up such a simple job! He did it fine last year—no problem. Tango had left everything in order; all Swing had to do was follow what had worked in the past.

The performers were now on official strike because Salsa was so impatient with them and couldn't keep quiet during rehearsals. Waltz tried to tell him how easy it is to sit in the audience and quietly listen to what was happening on stage, giving notes to the director for him to handle. Waltz couldn't understand how anybody could mess up such an easy job!

And speaking of Waltz, when the other twins realized that most of the work was being done by Waltz himself, instead of being delegated to others, they knew that at the rate Waltz was going, the festival was bound to open three months late. Salsa yelled at Waltz and said, "Why don't you just figure out who can do what, and then just tell them what to do! Don't procrastinate, just do it now!" Salsa couldn't understand how anybody could mess up such an easy job!

By now everyone was getting more upset by the minute. All the twins were seething with anger and frustration. Then it was Tango's turn to report how his committee was doing. Everybody had already heard how bad he was as the ringmaster. Swing said loudly, "All you have to do is wing it! You don't have to plan out every word. Just get up there and be funny! It's easy, just relax!" Swing couldn't understand how anybody could mess up such an easy job!

The tension in the room was getting as thick as the knot in a sailor's stomach anxious to avoid the slithering, sea serpent. Nobody noticed Discord the Intolerant in the back of the room, surveying his glorious creation of chaos. He was smiling his sly smile and slowly stroking his swishing, scarlet tail.

Each twin couldn't understand that if he could do the job just fine last year, why couldn't his current replacement do the same?

The argument escalated into a full-blown yelling match with everyone, even Waltz, shouting in a loud voice at exactly the same time "What's wrong with all of you? **Why can't everyone be like me?**"

In that instant, everything came to a standstill. The Crescendo River stopped flowing, and all became deathly silent. Each twin stopped in his tracks. They started to speak, when all of a sudden they vanished into thin air, leaving the rest of the royal subjects standing there in astonishment.

Chapter Six

IN A PERFECT WORLD EVERYONE IS JUST LIKE ME!

The desire was so strong, and their wish so intense, that in fact, each twin was magically transported to a separate world where everyone *was* exactly like them. Each was part of his own kingdom where everybody thought and acted just like him. And like many wishes come true, at first it seemed like heaven on earth because nobody saw the warning signs.

SWINGLAND

"Ouch! What in the world?" Swing squealed in pain. He looked around as he landed on a huge pile of keys. Little keys. Big keys. House keys, car keys, every kind of key imaginable was piled high, making a little mountain of cold, pointy projectiles. No wonder it hurt when Swing landed right on top of them.

Swing felt exhilarated, if not startled, by his journey to this most bizarre place. He couldn't understand what had happened, and where in the world he was. The last thing Swing remembered was arguing with the other twins about the annual festival. But even that thought was quickly fading.

"How did *you* get here?" Swing said out loud to his silent, iron companions, hoping to unlock the mystery. He looked around the huge building and gingerly navigated his way down the pointy mound of metal. There were other large piles of keys just like this one.

Walking outside, Swing was delighted to see something quite familiar—a tree house! In fact, throughout the land he saw hundreds, if not thousands, of all different kinds of tree houses!

"Hi! What's your name?" a happy voice asked Swing as he emerged from the gigantic building of keys. Before he could answer, the voice continued, "Are you on your way to the all-day festival uptown? I'm going, and I can't wait to play all the new games!" Swing joined his new friend and off they went. However, he was in such a hurry, that he didn't notice a sign over the door: "Lost & Found—Key Building." Swing also didn't notice another sign: Warning! Silence and organization are forbidden in this land!

WALTZLAND

The smell of fresh coffee greeted Waltz when he sleepily woke up to the gentle songs of the morning birds. The soft, feather bed lulled him to linger a while longer. When the aroma was joined by the smell of cinnamon rolls, it was too much. It finally motivated Waltz to lumber out of his soft sanctuary.

It wasn't until he walked into the kitchen that Waltz realized he wasn't in his own home. It felt like home, smelled like home, even looked like home. But looking out the heart-shaped window over the sink, he could see many other cottages that looked exactly like his. This was not the Mountains of Tranquillity. Then he vaguely remembered the fight he had had with the other twins—and their wish.

Waltz was greatly disturbed at this disruption in his routine. He didn't like change, especially when he was transported to some unknown realm where he had no idea where he was. So far, however, the peaceful surroundings, smells of breakfast, and the softest bed he ever slept on made the transition much easier. When Waltz stepped outside to breathe in the morning air, he didn't notice a sign that read: Warning! It is against the law of the land to utter the word, "No."

SALSALAND

"Ah, I love the smell of sawdust in the morning!" Salsa exclaimed as he surveyed new construction all around him. Nothing exhilarated Salsa more than the beginning a new project, if not the beginning of three new projects, or more!

Salsa usually had others do most of the detailed work. He was the one to come up with a grand scheme and plot it all out. He then expected others to carry out most the details of that plan.

He looked around at his new surroundings and loved what he saw. New construction was booming everywhere. All stores were open twenty-four hours a day, so that production would not be slowed down for an instant. If anyone ran out of supplies, no matter what the time, they could easily get what they needed to complete their project.

Salsa noticed he had on a new suit with all the latest efficiency, timesaving gadgets. Next to his polished black Italian leather shoes were his briefcase, palm pilot, pager, cell-phone, laptop, and portable fax machine. He was armed and ready to conquer this new world and relished the challenge set before him. Salsa was so caught up with his new kingdom, that he didn't notice a huge sign that read: Warning! It is against the law to say the words, "I'm sorry."

TANGOLAND

"N.S.F., I wonder what that is," said the bank president, examining the contents of the ancient bank vault.

"Non-sufficient-funds," replied the old security guard. "This was a common occurrence among the people who came before us."

The bank president just shook his head and wondered aloud how anybody could let their account go below zero. Everybody in Tangoland balanced their checkbook to the penny the day they received their bank statement. "How silly our ancestors were," said the president, "and how imperfect."

Tango overheard this fascinating conversation as he found himself in the lobby of an immaculately clean, organized bank: Fidelity Trust—Perfection in Finance. People were quietly waiting in line. At the end of the line, a computer screen announced the average waiting time: 1.47 minutes.

The soothing sounds of a string quartet greeted the customers during their lunch hour. Beautifully painted posters decorated the walls. They promoted the land's upcoming community events: poems by Plato, philosophical discussions by Aristotle, and the unveiling of Spock's latest scientific inventions.

Tango stepped out of line, wondering how he had gotten here. He didn't like to have his routine changed, even if it did bring him to such an orderly place.

He walked out of the bank and saw a stunning landscape: thousands of palaces with perfectly manicured lawns and gardens. The stores opened precisely at 7:59 a.m. and closed at precisely 4:59 p.m. Everyone was polite, respectful, and courteous.

Why Can't Everyone Be Like Me?

Tango had to admit that even though he hated change with no proven outcome, he did find this land of order a comfort after his harrowing experience with the festival planning. However, he didn't notice a small sign in the bank that read: Warning! It is against the law to utter the words, "I'm wrong."

Where had they landed? In a place where everyone was just like them. So, therefore the strengths that were part of each land were the only strengths throughout the kingdom. Because of this, trouble began to brew. These same strengths, when taken to the extreme, became weaknesses. And that led to disaster.

BE CAREFUL WHAT YOU WISH FOR…

EVERYONE IS JUST LIKE ME, SO WHAT COULD GO WRONG?

What occurred next was so horrible, that nobody ever knew exactly what had happened because the twins vowed never to dwell on such negatives again. Bits and pieces of stories that follow, however, are the ones that have survived over the years.

In Waltzland, everyone slowly worked themselves into exhaustion. Because it was against the law to say the words, "no" to anything—nobody could refuse a request. People became stressed out trying to accommodate everyone. However, many times, just because they *said* yes, that didn't mean they actually had to follow through on the promise, either. Chaos started to infect this peaceful land, because nobody could count on each other. People just smiled and said, "Oh, yes, I can do that. I'll be there," having no intention of going. Everyone also worried so much that they became depressed and overwhelmed. The Waltzland hospitals were over-run with cases of depression and ulcers because nobody wanted to talk about their problems or take any action to fix them.

Swingland was another chaotic disaster. Since silence and organization were banned, the entire land was so loud and messy, that eventually nobody wanted to venture out. All the festive parties that had once been so much fun, was now just a disorganized, loud jumble of people, causing Swingland's citizens to yell at each other with impatient demands. The tension was getting out of hand, and the hospitals were overflowing with cases of hearing loss, headaches, and panic attacks. And because organization was banned, the hospitals frequently made disastrous mistakes that cost people their lives.

In the kingdom where Salsa was, things started falling apart immediately. Since it was against the law to utter the words "I'm sorry," conflicts were never resolved and justice was never served. Everyone walked around absorbed in bitterness and unresolved resentments towards the people that hurt them. Negative feelings ran so deep, and everyone worked so much, that heart attacks afflicted huge numbers of people. It got so bad with everybody struggling for control, that civil war broke out, killing thousands.

Tangoland was the most depressing land of all. What started out as an orderly place, quickly became a perfectionistic nightmare. At one point, everyone wanted Tango to have brown eyes because that was deemed the perfect eye color. Tango had blue eyes. Since he could never achieve the perfect color, he was forever depressed. Striving for the impossible became his obsession. This fit in with the rest of the people, as they became obsessive/compulsive about every tiny detail. Since it was against the law to utter the words, "I'm wrong," and they were not perfect, therefore everyone was striving to achieve the impossible. Depression soon took over the land. It got so bad when the suicide rate increased, that funeral homes were the best financial investment in the land. Tangoland was becoming a ghost town.

WHAT WAS MISSING IN EACH LAND WAS IMPORTANT, TOO.

A WORLD WITHOUT WALTZ

It is also important to describe what *wasn't* in each of their lands. In the worlds without Waltz, war waged constantly. Nobody was good at being a diplomat, so conflict escalated throughout the land. Understanding and compassion were scarce. Others in the land failed to thrive because they didn't have the incredible supportive energy that Waltz usually gave them. Teamwork was lacking because there was no one who was good at listening to others' points of view. People in the land became depressed, because no one like Waltz was there to really care about them and lift them up.

A WORLD WITHOUT TANGO

All the lands except Tangoland, had very limited and poor quality technology. Something as simple as a light bulb wasn't yet perfected. Nobody had the patience of Tango to try thousands of experiments to do things right. Nobody had the detailed mind that Tango had, so they couldn't comprehend the very precise plans for complicated devices. For instance, flying machines would break down frequently, and people would die as a result.

Most everything was done by hand, which left the way open to error. And because nobody had the patience to plan out very detailed artwork, there were no beautifully painted ceilings on chapels, and statues were crude and not magnificent. And speaking of people dying, because nobody had the desire to strive for perfection, the medical field was also sorely lacking in expertise. The doctors of the land had finally mastered how to operate on their subjects, but very precise procedures failed miserably.

Why Can't Everyone Be Like Me?

A WORLD WITHOUT SWING

On the other hand, the worlds without Swing were dismal at best. The sun hardly ever shone in these kingdoms. It rained a lot, but there was never a rainbow. The energy was low or serious, not much fun ever happened, as laughter was in short supply. There was no happy excitement. No plays or comedies were presented, as there was no one who really loved being up on stage. There were no festive parties or vacations. The worlds without Swing were gray and dismal.

A WORLD WITHOUT SALSA

In the worlds without Salsa, there were no grand events or buildings. There was no drive or ambition to strive for the best. The countries within the kingdoms were not run efficiently, because nobody wanted to take on such an enormous responsibility. Nobody liked conflict, so disputes abounded without being resolved.

And speaking of no big events, the Olympics didn't exist in the worlds without Salsa. Nobody could conceive of such a grandiose plan that took such huge amounts of energy and planning. In fact, nobody had big dreams, goals, or vision.

THERE'S NO PLACE LIKE HOME.

One by one, Waltz, Tango, Swing, and Salsa wearied with everyone in their new kingdoms. In fact, all the worlds were now crumbling around them. The twins finally realized that having a world where everyone was just like them was not at all what they had expected. They needed each other and the others' special talents to make their lives complete. They missed the differences in each twin, and even started to chuckle at the others' weaknesses. The other's defects of character weren't so bad after all, they thought. So they each embarked on a journey to try and find their way home.

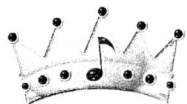

CHAPTER SEVEN

THE JOURNEY HOME – FOUR KEYS TO THE HARMONY PRINCIPLE

ASKING FOR HELP AND ADMITTING YOUR FAULTS. (CHARACTER WEAKNESSES)

SALSA WANTED IT NOW!

Salsa, of course, barged ahead on a path of paved yellow bricks. This turned out to be a dead end. All he found was an old wizard who lived in an emerald house. He was a kind and wise wizard who suggested to Salsa that he ask for help in finding his way home. The mere thought of asking for help was appalling to Salsa. He considered himself extremely competent and had overcome many things in his life. Salsa didn't need anybody.

WALTZ WANTED THE WAY HOME TO BE EASY.

Waltz wanted the way back to be easy. He found what he thought was a magical turtle because it was dressed in a tuxedo! He picked up the little green fellow and repeated an incantation he had heard long ago: "Dweezle, dwazzle, dwizzle, dome, time for this one to go home!" The turtle just stuck his head out, looked at Waltz and squirmed off his hand. Waltz didn't budge a bit.

TANGO HAD PARALYSIS BY ANALYSIS.

Tango spent hour upon hour meticulously plotting his escape route, including how much food he would need along the way. He agonized over every detail. He wanted to get going, but decided to keep planning, just in case a certain aspect of the trip wasn't perfect. He came up with several "what if" scenarios for each situation and tried to anticipate a primary, secondary, and back-up plan for unforeseen situations. He was getting more anxious to leave, but was paralyzed by so much analysis. This made him even more depressed. He was stuck.

SWING IMPULSIVELY STOMPED OFF!

In contrast, Swing just decided one morning, after a very chaotic experience he had trying to put on a party, that he had had enough! He started out the east gate of Swingland to what he thought might be the way home. He was angry and impulsively stomped off. It wasn't until he got outside the city limits, that he discovered he hadn't planned a thing! Now he was hungry and had no food except for a few melted chocolates still left in his pocket from the ill-fated party.

"Help, I need somebody. Help, not just anybody."

THE OTHER "ROYAL QUARTET"—THE BEATLES

HELP IS ON THE WAY... JUST ASK FOR IT

Finally, Waltz, Tango, Swing, and Salsa all became weary of trying to go home on their own. Each one, in his own way, finally cried out for help. Each one started to realize how his faults had caused so much trouble for himself and others. Each one realized that he needed help to get out of this mess. Only then did any of them start making progress on their journey home.

Strengths, when taken to the extreme, become weaknesses.

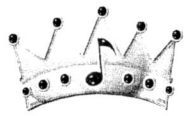

Your Personality Kingdom™
Like four part harmony, each personality is needed.

WALTZ'S WANDERINGS

Waltz did not want to go at first, even though he didn't especially like where he was, he didn't like thinking of making another change either. He admitted that he had to work on his weaknesses—lack of motivation and indecision. He had seen, when he was surrounded by people just like him, how annoying, and just plain ineffective these traits could be. Just then, a scroll appeared with a list of possible character defects for Waltz. He learned that he had to work on the following weaknesses:

"I've suffered a great many catastrophes in my life.

Most of them never happened."

MARK TWAIN

WALTZ THE WARM-HEARTED POSSIBLE CHARACTER WEAKNESSES

Acquiesce (give in)	Absent-minded
Avoids responsibility	Apathetic
Bashful	Cluttered
Depressed	Disorganized
Doubtful	Fearful
Late	Indecisive
Martyr	Lazy
Others more important	Passive
Passive/aggressive	Quiet will of steel
Poor self-esteem	Self-righteous

Says yes, means no	Stubborn
Slow	Stuck in rut
Sluggish	Two-faced
Unenthusiastic	Unmotivated
Worrier	Wishy-washy

Waltz pondered these things, and remembered one time when he waited so long to make a decision, the opportunity was gone! He remembered many times when he had acted in such a wishy-washy way. Waltz gave a sigh of relief when he admitted his faults. Then a surge of energy came over him. He realized that some of the negative outcomes were the direct result of his own thinking and actions—or lack of actions, which was most often the case. If that were true, then he realized he had the power to choose different actions and create different outcomes the next time! Nice!

He also remembered trying to be outgoing and loud, something he was not. He remembered wishing he were someone else and loathing his shy personality. Just then a light, soft musical note was heard and a magical key appeared before him that was inscribed:

KEY #1 – LIKE A SONG OF FOUR-PART HARMONY,

EVERY PERSONALITY KINGDOM IS NEEDED.

Waltz reached for the magic key. When he closed his fingers around it, poof! He vanished with the wind.

TANGO'S TRIP

Tango did not like the change to his new world either. But he slowly learned that it was illogical to expect perfection in people, and he should instead strive for excellence when dealing with people and especially with himself! He also learned that he had to work on his other personality weaknesses. Tango saw a scroll that had a long list of character weaknesses.

> *"One of my problems is that I internalize everything. I can't express anger. I grow a tumor instead."*
>
> WOODY ALLEN

TANGO THE THINKER—POSSIBLE CHARACTER WEAKNESSES

Bogged down in planning	Caught up in details
Can't say "I'm wrong"	Critical
Cheap, too frugal	Demands perfection
Hard on self	False humility
Hyper sensitive	Fussy, picky
Hypochondriac	Hard to get moving
Insecure	Not a team player
Isolated	Obsessive-compulsive
Low self-image	Pessimistic
Perfectionist	Poor social skills
Resentful	Self-righteous
Sets impossible standards	Slow to act
Takes things personally	Stubborn
Tends toward depression	Too emotional
Unforgiving	Withdrawn

Tango realized that he was free to make mistakes. He did not have to expect perfection in himself or others. He was determined to never return to the perfectionistic realm of Tangoland. He practiced saying the words, "I'm wrong" over and over so that he could say them to the people he cared for most.

In a perfect world, we would only have the strengths of each Personality Kingdom, and none of the weaknesses!

Your Personality Kingdom™
Like four part harmony, each personality is needed.

Tango realized that the desire to strive for excellence gave him his ability to analyze things and think deep thoughts. Perfectionism, and striving for the impossible, was something he reverted to when he wasn't quite right with himself. Being able to recognize his personality style was powerful to Tango. Knowing that he had special talents made Tango feel valuable. Knowing that he was prone to certain negative behaviors made it easier to fix those ineffective qualities!

Just then, melancholy sounding music, like a Cello, pierced the quiet, black night, and the same kind of key that Waltz found, now appeared before him. This inscription on the key read:

KEY #2—TREASURE YOUR PERSONALITY KINGDOM,

KNOW HOW YOU DANCE THROUGH LIFE.

Tango reached for the key, closed his fingers around it, and just like Waltz vanished into thin air.

SALSA'S STRUGGLE

Salsa loved change and welcomed the adventure of the unknown journey back. He learned to stop and smell the roses and not be so intense about everything. Salsa learned how bad it feels to be bossed around all the time, as he especially hated being *told* what to do instead of being *asked*. It seemed like a small thing, but it had great implications. The message was, "You don't count! You are not important enough to take into consideration. Only *my* feelings are worthy!" Salsa thought back to how often he had hurt his friends with his harsh words and curt manner. A scroll, like the others found, now appeared with a list of possible character flaws. Salsa knew he had to work on these faults:

"...Never will I allow myself to become so impatient, so wise, so dignified, so powerful, that I forget how to laugh at myself and my world..."

FROM THE SCROLL MARKED VII
OG MANDINO—THE GREATEST SALESMAN IN THE WORLD

SALSA THE SUPREME—POSSIBLE CHARACTER WEAKNESSES

Aggressive	Bursts of rage
Argumentative	Cold, unemotional
Arrogant	Comes on too strong
Blunt	Controlling
Bossy	Crafty, manipulative
Can do everything better	Cruel
Can't relax	Domineering
Can't say, "I'm sorry"	End justifies the means
Decides for others	Impatient
Demanding	Inflexible, rigid
Know-it-all attitude	Interrupts
Negative, sarcastic	Not sensitive to others
Short-tempered	Rude
Stubborn	Tactless
Unaffectionate	Workaholic

Admitting your faults can be life changing, because you only have the power to change yourself.

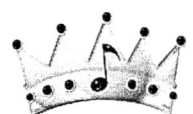

Your Personality Kingdom™
Like four part harmony, each personality is needed.

"Rudeness is the weak man's imitation of strength."

Eric Hoffer

Salsa hated to admit that he had any faults, let alone the dreaded possibility that he may have many! But he was determined to leave Salsaland and all its intensity. He actually had to practice saying the words, "I'm sorry," because he had never uttered them in his entire life. When he did, a deep musical note, like a string bass, sounded throughout the land, and a key appeared before him, which was inscribed:

KEY #3 – KNOW HOW YOUR ACTIONS AFFECT OTHERS.

Like the others, Salsa reached for the key, and held it tight. When he did, he, too, disappeared.

SWING'S SURRENDER

Swing loved the adventure of leaving. He couldn't wait to meet all sorts of new people along his journey. He learned, though, that everybody talking all the time about themselves was really quite selfish. He also saw how chaotic life gets when everybody loses things all the time! Swing learned to stop and listen to the cool mountain streams and just "be." He learned that he could stop and take a breath.

He also learned that being silent was really quite nice. Swing thought back to all the times that he interrupted other people. Swing thought about the time he hurt Tango's feelings by not appreciating the excellent job he had done designing his spiral slide.

Swing pondered on these possible negatives that appeared to him on a scroll.

"I'm talking and I can't shut up!"

ANONYMOUS

SWING THE STAR—POSSIBLE CHARACTER WEAKNESSES

Angered easily	Childish
Answers for others	Doesn't finish projects
Cluttered	Easily distracted
Disorganized	Egotistical
Dominates conversations	Fickle, unstable
Exaggerates stories	Impulsive
Forgetful	Interrupts
Hates to be alone	Invasive of other's space
Hyper, restless energy	Losses things
Loud voice and laugh	Not time oriented
Poor follow-through	Scatterbrained
Shallow	Seems insincere
Show-off	Talks too much
Superficial	Too dramatic
Unproductive	Undisciplined

Swing was so excited! It actually felt good to admit his faults. Then a peaceful feeling came over him that he had never felt before. Swing realized that he couldn't change who he was but he certainly could change his words and actions to be in tune with others.

Finally, when Swing accepted that he had many faults, a sweet happy tone came from within the birch trees, and a magical key appeared before him, which was inscribed:

KEY #4 -- ADJUST YOUR ACTIONS TO BE IN TUNE WITH OTHERS.

TREAT PEOPLE THE WAY *THEY* WANT TO BE TREATED.

Swing grabbed the key, and vanished just like the others had.

Each twin had to take a long, hard look at their weaknesses and had to admit that they did have some of these negative traits. They also discovered that when they were feeling bad about themselves or were tired or hungry, sick or stressed out, the negative traits were more apt to appear.

The chaotic land of Swingland, the perfectionist realm of Tangoland, the sluggish kingdom of Waltzland, and the intense valley of Salsaland were places the twins would never forget. They took with them their Scrolls of Shortcomings and strove to minimize these defects of character whenever possible.

Negative personality traits are more apt to appear when you are feeling tired, hungry, sick or stressed out.

Your Personality Kingdom™
Like four part harmony, each personality is needed.

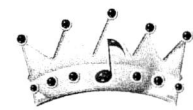

Chapter Eight

The Magic Box – Back at The Crescendo River

Waltz, Tango, Swing, and Salsa find their way home!

Meanwhile, mysterious happenings were brewing over The Crescendo River. Recently, sections of a bridge had begun to appear, which connected each kingdom to a central portico over the middle of the great rushing Crescendo River.

One sunny morning Waltz, Tango, Swing, and Salsa suddenly appeared in the center of this bridge which now connected all four kingdoms together. Startled, weary, yet overjoyed at the realization that they were finally home, they all embraced each other and cried tears of joy.

Then The Royal Quartet noticed an old wooden box in the center of the bridge. It looked like their keys might fit the four keyholes. In turn, each took out his key and shared what he had learned, which turned out to be the Four Keys to **The Harmony Principle**:

FOUR KEYS TO THE HARMONY PRINCIPLE

KEY #1 – LIKE A SONG OF FOUR-PART HARMONY,

    EACH PERSONALITY KINGDOM IS NEEDED.

KEY #2 – TREASURE YOUR PERSONALITY KINGDOM–

    KNOW HOW YOU DANCE THROUGH LIFE.

KEY #3 – KNOW HOW YOUR ACTIONS AFFECT OTHERS.

KEY #4 – ADJUST YOUR ACTIONS TO BE IN TUNE WITH OTHERS.

    TREAT PEOPLE THE WAY *THEY* WANT TO BE TREATED.

When the last key was in, Waltz, Tango, Swing, and Salsa looked at each other, not sure what would happen next. All at the same time, they turned the keys. Click! Just then, two strange humming sounds came from the distant Mountains of Tranquillity. One was a slow, light and flowing flute, and the other was the deep mellow sound of a cello. These notes began to swirl together with two other musical tones that came from The Sea of Adventure. One sounded bright, fast and intense like a violin. The other was the deep, strong sound of a string bass. When these beautiful sounds finally came together at the new Center Bridge, there was a brilliant light.

Now there were four, distinct sounds all swirling together, making the most beautiful music the land had ever heard. Then, with a loud thunderclap from the wooden box, out flew a shimmering faerie!

With the harmonious music still hanging in the air, the twins turned to the faerie and asked who she was. She replied not with an answer but with a command for The Royal Quartet to sing a song of celebration. "We cannot sing like we used to, for we must be enchanted," they answered ashamed.

Why Can't Everyone Be Like Me?

"Fools!" she said, "Do as I say! Are you not delighted to be back home and have new insights into your life? You see, every time you admitted your character faults and found a key to **The Harmony Principle**, one section of the bridge was built from your kingdom to connect all the other kingdoms together." Then, they slowly started to sing, and surprisingly, out came the most beautiful four-part harmony they had ever sung. For now that they had accepted themselves and others, they were free to be the best person they could be. They would not try to be like someone else, or force others to be like them.

Pointing a finger at Discord the Intolerant, the faerie broke the spell, "Discord the Intolerant, you are forever banned from this land! Now the enchantment is over. Let the festival begin, for I am Perfect Harmony, guardian of the land."

Discord the Intolerant slipped away into the Valley of Despair, forever banned from The Land of Harmony.

The End of The Legend: *Why Can't Everyone Be Like Me?*

Now we know why everyone can't be the same!

Great Aunt Nana concluded her story with a dramatic bow. She slowly closed the creaky storybook, and gracefully replaced the leather straps of the little wooden chest, deciding not to share those contents just yet. Wendy, Thomas, Suzi, and Sergio were amazed, if not a little overwhelmed with all the new information they had to process. As the fire and candles flickered for the last time, they went upstairs to get a good night's sleep.

Now that you have accepted yourself and others, you are free to be the best person you can be; not trying to be like someone else, or forcing others to be like you.

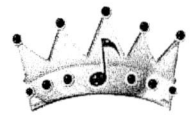

Your Personality Kingdom™
Like four part harmony, each personality is needed.

Part Three

Benefits
of
The Harmony Principle

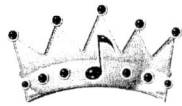

CHAPTER NINE

SOLUTIONS TO MODERN PROBLEMS

BENEFITS OF APPLYING

THE FOUR KEYS TO THE HARMONY PRINCIPLE

In the morning, Wendy, Thomas, Suzi, and Sergio woke up early. They were anxious to apply The Legend to their problems they had discussed the night before. Over hot coffee and cinnamon rolls, the four friends talked about which kingdom they might belong to—how did they dance through life? They each took turns telling how he or she could see themselves in one of The Personality Kingdoms.

Great Aunt Nana explained that most people have character traits from each kingdom, and some people are a combination of styles. Sometimes people are more from one kingdom at work and a different one at home. Also some people seem to change somewhat over the years. So the question became, what is your *predominate* Personality Kingdom? What would be your reaction *most* of the time? Great Aunt

Nana also explained that a person didn't need to have all of the positive or negative traits to be from a certain Personality Kingdom.

In fact, it was quite easy. The four friends determined what Personality Kingdom they were from in just two steps. Just like in the story, they had to see where they lived on The Crescendo River of Energy.

First, they asked themselves if they were from The Family of Introvert or Extrovert. The Family of Introvert was shy, quiet and low-key. The Family of Extrovert was out-going, high-energy and loud. Then, they asked themselves what side of the river do they usually live on: the Thinking side–the East Coast, where people like to have planned structure, or the Feeling side–the West Coast, where people were more laid-back and flexible.

In reviewing the personality strengths and weakness traits, using the word "or" seemed to help. The question wasn't, "Am I this trait?" But, rather, "Am I more this trait *or* another trait from a different kingdom?" Also asking each other how others perceived them was very helpful in getting a clear picture of themselves.

It's easy to determine what Personality Kingdom you are from. You just need to see where you live on The Crescendo River of Energy.

Shared Personality Traits
Introvert or Extrovert Family

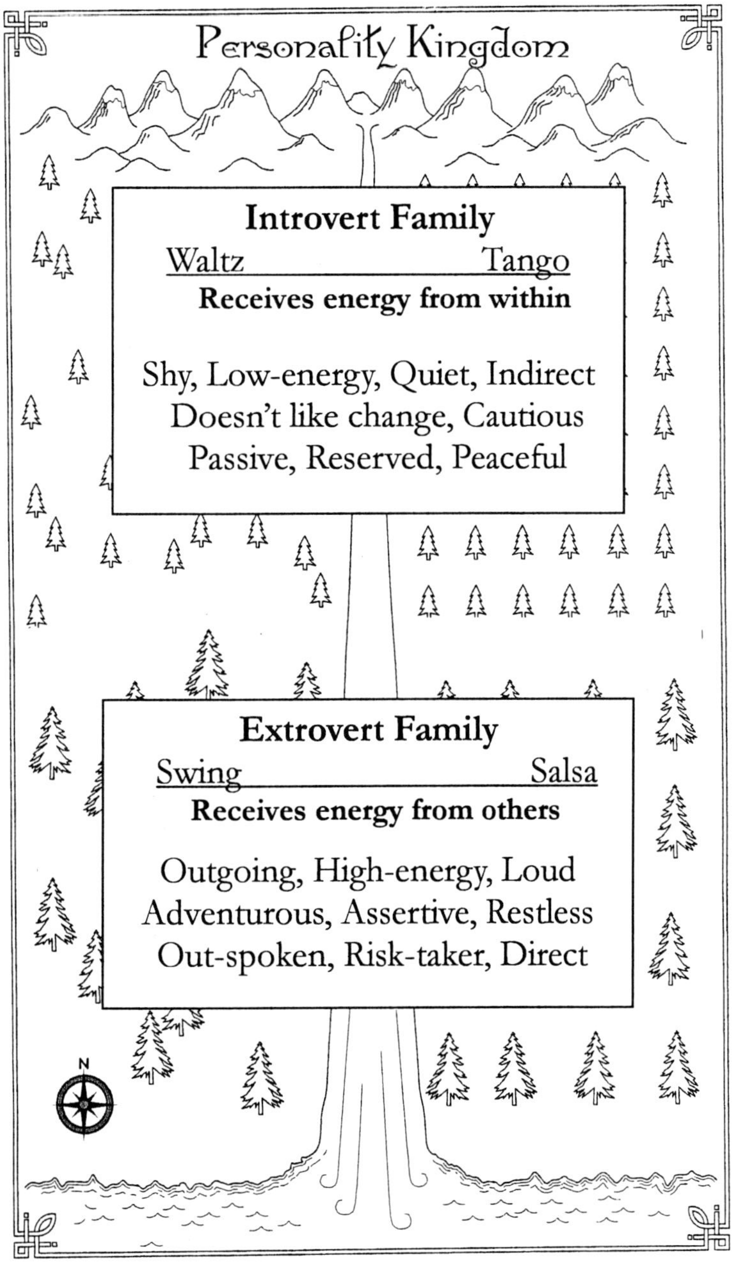

Personality Kingdom

Introvert Family

Waltz ——— Tango

Receives energy from within

Shy, Low-energy, Quiet, Indirect
Doesn't like change, Cautious
Passive, Reserved, Peaceful

Extrovert Family

Swing ——— Salsa

Receives energy from others

Outgoing, High-energy, Loud
Adventurous, Assertive, Restless
Out-spoken, Risk-taker, Direct

Shared Personality Traits
Feeling or Thinking Outlook

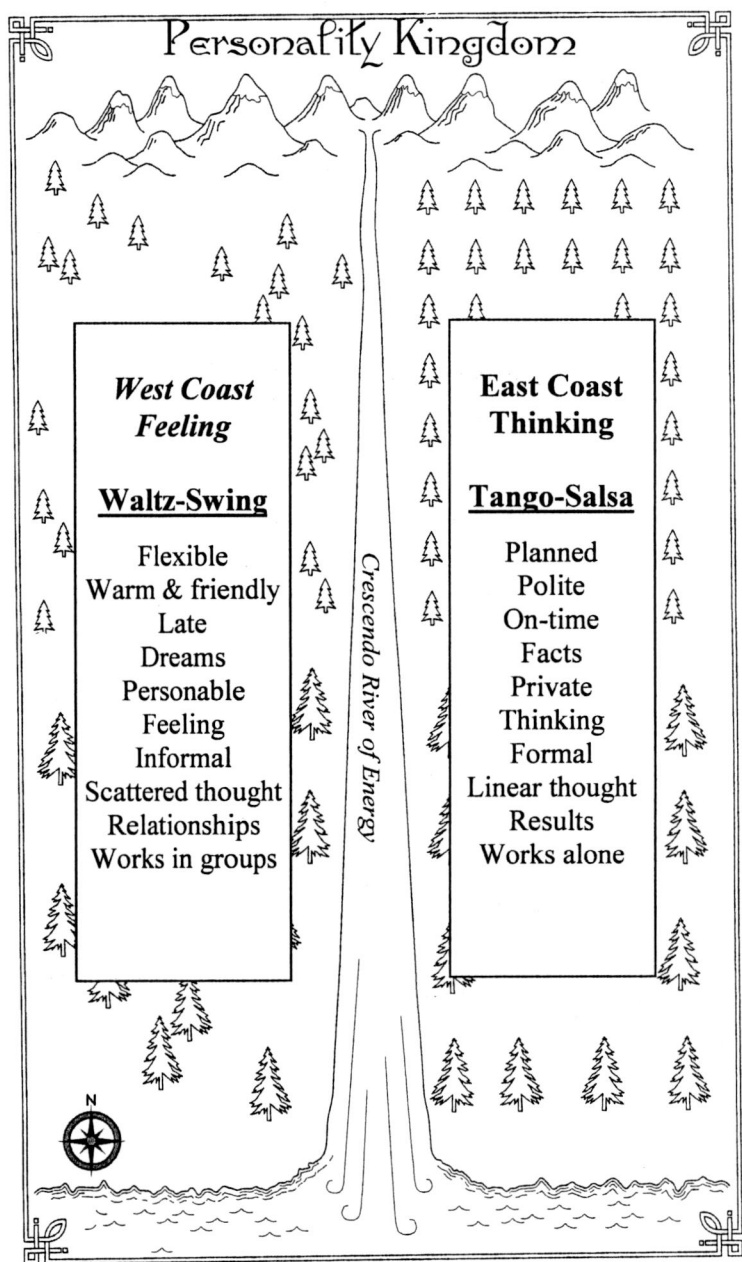

Why Can't Everyone Be Like Me?

Suzi determined that she was Extroverted and Feeling, so she must be from the Swing Kingdom because she loved to have fun all the time! Sergio said he was Extroverted and Thinking so he was from the Salsa Kingdom as he really enjoyed accomplishing as much as possible. Thomas was hesitant to come to a determination, needing all of the facts first, but he liked thinking about living in Tango's Palace with all of its perfection. He finally decided that he was more Introverted and Thinking so he was from the Tango Kingdom. Wendy loved Waltz the Warm-Hearted because she pictured herself high up in the Mountains of Tranquillity sitting in The Royal Cottage with friends. Because Wendy was Introverted and Feeling, she concluded that she was from the Waltz Kingdom.

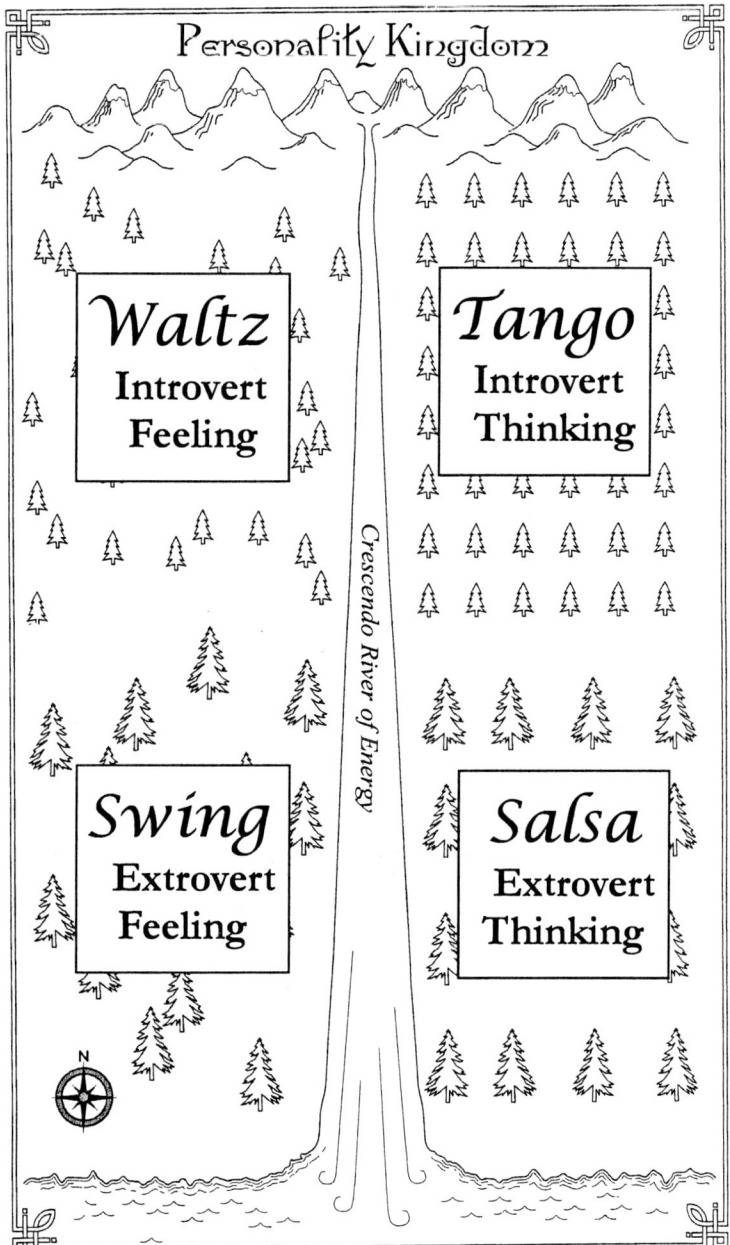

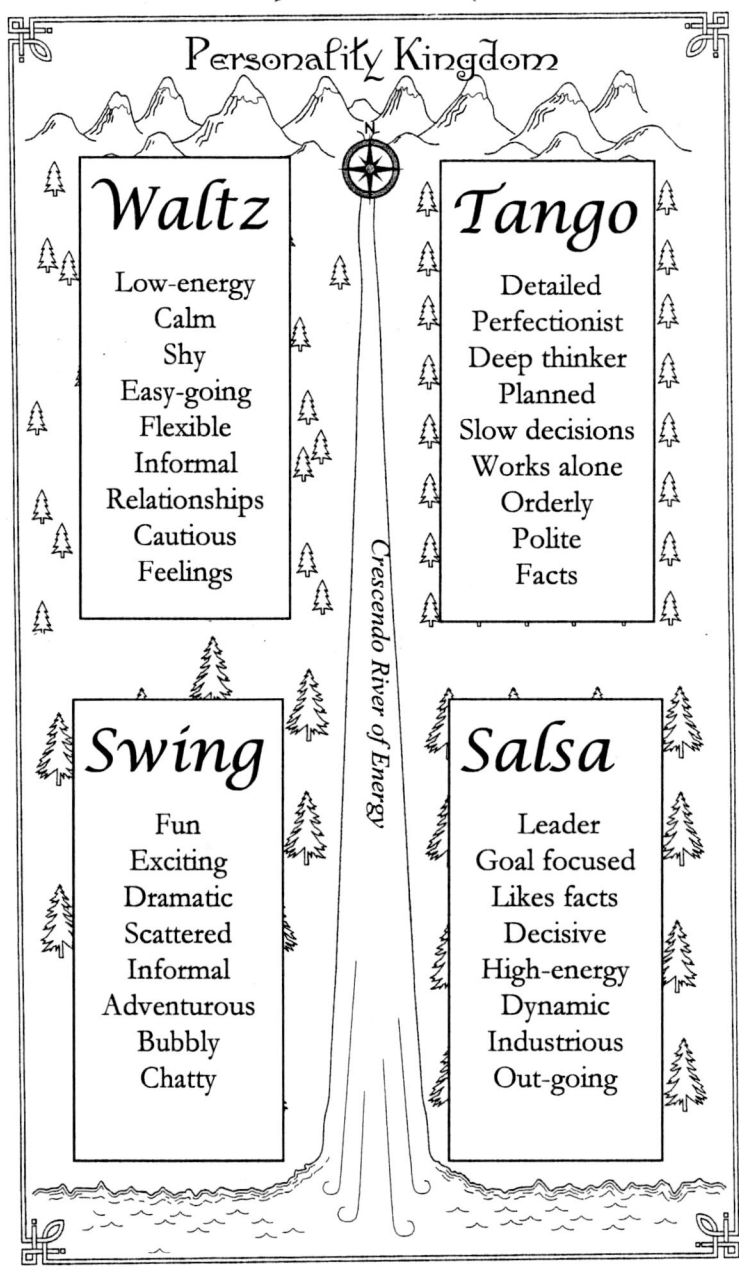

Wendy, Thomas, Suzi, and Sergio all went back to their jobs, family, and school to start applying the Four Keys to **The Harmony Principle**.

KEY #1 -- LIKE A SONG OF FOUR-PART HARMONY,

EACH PERSONALITY KINGDOM IS NEEDED.

BENEFIT: SAVE TIME AND ENERGY BY ACCEPTING,

YOURSELF AND OTHERS AS THEY ARE!

Thomas told his father about The Legend. He could tell that his dad was from the Salsa Kingdom, so he used words and phrases that were Music To His Ears. He got right to the point and told his dad that the way he'd been forcing his personality style on Thomas was counter-productive to his dad's own goals! He told his father that it would take only a short time to hear the whole story and that it would be worth his time. It was.

Thomas's father was shocked to find out just how much it had hurt his son to be pushed into something that was against his basic nature. Trying to force his son, to be something he was not, was just like forcing himself to have low-energy, be silent in strategic planning sessions, and become an introvert instead of his naturally outgoing self. These new thoughts took time to sink in, but finally Thomas' father understood and appreciated his son.

KEY #2 -- TREASURE YOUR PERSONALITY KINGDOM—
KNOW HOW YOU DANCE THROUGH LIFE.

BENEFIT: ACCEPTING WHO YOU ARE,

INCREASES SELF-ESTEEM.

As for Wendy, she actually said "no" to a request for yet another committee and didn't even feel guilty about it. She also realized that she had to directly tell her husband when he was wearing her out with his demands. He really did want to protect her–but he wasn't a mind reader either.

Wendy also began to understand and accept her shy personality style. She started to see how valuable she was even though she was more low-key than her friends were. Up until now, she secretly loathed her shy personality, and even took classes to make her more outgoing. But after hearing The Legend, Wendy realized that what she really needed was confidence in herself as an important part of a team. When Wendy thought about how valuable Waltz the Warm-Hearted was in the kingdom, she smiled with pride as she saw herself from the Kingdom of Waltz.

KEY #3 – KNOW HOW YOUR ACTIONS AFFECT OTHERS.

BENEFIT: BEING AWARE CREATES AN ENVIRONMENT OF CARING.

At last, Suzi got her act together and realized how being late and disorganized all the time negatively affected her family and friends. She also realized that she was in the wrong career and joined Sergio on the sales force. Wanting to please her parents, Suzi became an accountant only because her mother did that kind of work. And besides, she was constantly correcting her mistakes. Now she knew why!

Instead of working all the time, Sergio learned how to prioritize his day so that he had quality time with the important people in his life. He also learned to accept his shy son and appreciate *his* unique strengths. Sergio even said he was sorry to his son, then he got a father's day card announcing that he was "The Best Dad Ever!"

KEY #4 – ADJUST YOUR ACTIONS TO BE IN TUNE WITH OTHERS.

TREAT OTHERS THE WAY *THEY* WANT TO BE TREATED.

BENEFIT: SPEAKING THE OTHER PERSON'S LANGUAGE IS THE KEY TO SUCCESS.

Suzi became the leading sales person at MicroSurf by changing her behavior to suit those of her prospects. She treated people the way *they* wanted to be treated: using words and phrases that were Music To My Ears. Suzi used to interact with people the way *she* wanted to be treated, now she was in tune with what mattered most to others.

When she dealt with high-powered decision-makers, Suzi knew she had to be fast-paced, to the point and said things like "bottom-line," and that this product would help them achieve "your important goals." Suzi knew people like this were from the Salsa Kingdom.

On the other hand, when Suzi went to call on a shy, low-key business owner, she really had to take a deep breath, and slow down. She asked about personal matters first, then talked about business. Suzi made sure that she used words like "good for relationships," "everybody benefits," and "easy to use." Suzi knew that this business owner appreciated being treated in an easy, relaxed manner because he was from the Kingdom of Waltz.

The next time Suzi visited her outgoing, best customer's office, she wasn't annoyed that he was late, again. She knew that this customer was from Swing's Kingdom and could tend to be disorganized. Suzi used words like, "fun," "exciting," and "fast" about the latest products. Suzi knew that her customer was an impulse buyer, who made decisions based on feelings. Therefore, she was also careful to make sure he really wanted the new products, so he wouldn't impulsively want to return them the next day!

And finally, Suzi knew that when she dealt with her accountant client she should be very accurate, and present him with all the facts. Suzi knew that he was from the Kingdom of Tango and needed plenty of time and data before making a decision. She used words like, "that's correct," "perfect," and "you are exactly right."

MANY OTHERS WANTED TO HEAR ABOUT THE HARMONY PRINCIPLE

Many others asked about **The Harmony Principle** so they could reap the benefits of this simple, yet far-reaching concept.

Wendy, Thomas, Suzi, and Sergio went back to Great Aunt Nana and asked if she had copies of The Legend. She said, "Yes, go to the library and get them." When they entered the massive library they were surprised to find it stacked full with copies of The Legend named *Why Can't Everyone Be Like Me?*, published by Celesta Pines Press. These books were under a section that read: *Book One in The Chronicles of Harmony*. They were overjoyed and went back to their work, school and homes with their stack of cherished books.

WORD SPREAD

Now everyone wanted to hear about **The Harmony Principle**. Co-workers at MicroSurf wanted to read about it to help them at work and in their personal lives. More and more people were talking about which Personality Kingdom they belonged to! It was so much fun to learn about the differences in people, and to learn about the things they all had in common, like wanting to be accepted for who they were.

THE ROYAL QUARTET

AN EASY WAY TO IDENTIFY PERSONALITY STYLE

Many people at MicroSurf had heard about the concept of different personality styles before, but some of them couldn't remember the terms and were confused by the test that had to be taken. The concept of The Royal Quartet was easy to understand. The employees put up posters of The Crescendo River on their walls. These posters *showed* the four Personality Kingdoms, so it was easier to visually tell where you fit in.

Using **The Harmony Principle** accomplished many things in the company. Understanding this concept was paramount for business and personal success. The vocabulary of The Personality Kingdoms was fun and easy to remember, so everyone enjoyed using it. And it was a unifying force that fostered high employee moral. It worked, and it was just plain fun!

BE IN TUNE WITH OTHERS

People were applying this principle of acceptance and tolerance, but not of excuses! They became "in tune" with each other:

T -- Tolerance

U -- Understanding

N -- No

E -- Excuses

The employees came up with this easy device because some people when they heard The Legend, used it as an excuse not to change: "See, I can't change, that's just the way I am," some would say. Which of course everybody knew was just an excuse for bad behavior!

Speaking the other person's language is the key to success and harmony.

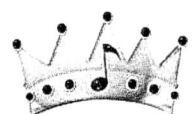

Your Personality Kingdom™
Like four part harmony, each personality is needed.

Why Can't Everyone Be Like Me?

THE HARMONY PRINCIPLE AT WORK

CREATING A BETTER WORKING ENVIRONMENT

Employees good-naturedly kidded each other about their differences. One time, the human resources manager breezed in and announced that she was from Swing's Tree House and that was why she was running late.

Because the four friends brought this fun and valuable tool to the workplace, they were now being called Wendy Waltz, Thomas Tango, Suzi Swing and Sergio Salsa!

EASIER CUSTOMER SERVICE

Customer service also became much easier. One of the first questions to ask in any situation was: How does this customer dance through life, what is his Personality Kingdom? Human resources included this question on their job applications.

For example, when a conservative, immaculately dressed customer slowly and deliberately walked into the customer service area saying his bill was incorrect, the employee knew right away that he was from the Tango Kingdom. She knew to stick with facts and figures and used as much time as necessary to explain the bill.

THE HARMONY PRINCIPLE AT HOME – SAVING MARRIAGES

People also took the book home and shared **The Harmony Principle** with their families. Marriages were saved as some frustrated couples finally realized that they instinctively chose mates from opposite Personality Kingdoms to complement their own personality style. Then they realized that the opposite strengths in their mates were what first attracted them to each other, even though they also had to live with the opposite weaknesses!

When couples started to value their different strengths, and not try to *change* each other, they achieved harmony in the home. It seemed like such a simple concept, yet applying it made all the difference.

Other couples who regularly experienced conflict realized that they had married within their same Personality Kingdom and were struggling for control—this was especially true of the Salsa Kingdom. They came to learn that any combination of personality styles could be happy, but that each partner would have their particular strengths and weaknesses. And each couple would have a unique combination of challenges. Knowing what to expect greatly reduced stress levels.

Understanding this concept finally brought light to some of their most troubling problems! Striving to understand and appreciate, instead of trying to change someone, worked like magic to create harmony in the home.

> *"Raise up a child in the way he should go."*
>
> PROVERBS 22:6

KEY #1 -- LIKE A SONG OF FOUR-PART HARMONY, EACH PERSONALITY KINGDOM IS NEEDED

Parents started to realize that their children might be different from them, and that was a good thing, too! They delighted in seeing a particular personality style crop up in their young children. When Suzi's quiet, four-year old nephew would organize his toy cars into categories and line them up into perfect rows, she knew he was probably from the Tango Kingdom. When her niece would giggle a lot and run around the room with lightning speed, Suzi knew she was from Swing's Tree House!

Parents learned that they needed to let their children be themselves. Period! Through reading the story of The Royal Quartet, they realized that everyone is born a particular way, and that no one style is better than the next. They knew that no matter how much a person tried to be something different, their natural instincts would creep through. And why not let these natural tendencies shine? However, that didn't mean you should let children run amuck. **The Harmony Principle** was not one of excuses! Simply put, every child has the right to be the person they were intended to be.

One time, over the holidays, Sergio decided to involve his family in understanding **The Harmony Principle** in a unique way. While they were seated around the fireplace, with the snow falling outside, a thought came to him. He led the older children and a few adults out of the room. He then handed them each a copy of *Why Can't Everyone Be Like Me?*, and gave them each a certain part of The Legend to read. They improvised costumes that matched each part and paraded back to their curious family and friends.

When they finished reading The Legend, they each took turns relating which Personality Kingdom they might belong to. They had so much fun, they hardly realized they were learning an important lesson about acceptance, understanding, and tolerance.

UNDERSTANDING IS THE KEY TO HARMONY

BENEFIT: KNOWING WHAT TO EXPECT FROM OTHERS, REDUCES STRESS.

People everywhere applied **The Harmony Principle** to their lives. They made better career decisions, students chose education majors that suited their personality, and families relaxed and had more fun together. Spouses also learned to let go of trying to change their mates. Singles learned how to choose partners based on personality style. By applying **The Harmony Principle,** everybody created more success and harmony in their lives.

The four friends delighted in helping people realize their own cherished goals. But what happened next, was something they never dreamed of.

Knowing what to expect from others reduces stress.

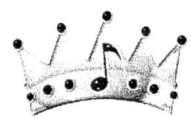

Your Personality Kingdom™
Like four part harmony, each personality is needed.

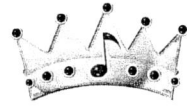

Chapter Ten

Success and the Magic Map

More and more people wanted to hear about **The Harmony Principle**. The demand for seminars and presentations was so great that Wendy, Thomas, Suzi, and Sergio eventually started their own company. The four friends continued to practice **The Harmony Principle** and the fruit of their efforts were realized in many ways.

Their business thrived, and so did their personal relationships. One relationship in particular was dear to them. After much thought, and planning, Thomas started to court the enchanting girl he met at The Victory Ball—Mona Lisa, or Lisa as she preferred. He applied **The Harmony Principle**, and gave up looking for "the perfect woman." The next year, the four friends returned to Celesta Pines Manor for the wedding of Thomas and Lisa.

As part of the festivities the four friends were invited to stay at Celesta Pines for the entire wedding weekend. Thomas and Lisa were treated to a special honeymoon cottage on the lush manor grounds.

Why Can't Everyone Be Like Me?

This time by the fire, all four friends reminisced about the previous year's success of their new company–Harmony 4 Personality Styles. The Legend was translated into many different languages as the dance theme, and ancient story, were very popular with people from all backgrounds and ages. It seemed that it was a topic that everyone wanted to know more about– themselves! In fact, this simple idea and one small book grew into a worldwide movement.

Another ambitious project was finally realized when Sergio secured land to re-create The Crescendo River kingdom. He thought it could be a magical training center, with each Royal House actually built around a central river. Counselors, teachers, and other speakers wanted to spread **The Harmony Principle** and put on presentations themselves. For training, they would come to this kingdom and stay in each Royal House.

At first they were anxious about starting such a huge venture. But then they all laughed and realized that each of them represented one of The Four Personality Kingdoms. If they applied **The Harmony Principle** to their business venture, they would do just fine! They each went into the part of the business that naturally suited their strengths. Sergio was the director, Thomas was the accountant and oversaw all artwork, Suzi was the vice president of sales, and Wendy was the head administrator.

The business was a smashing success and they were all extremely happy that they could realize some of their dreams of financial security and helping people they loved. It had indeed been a successful year and all were very grateful.

During the wedding weekend, they were awakened in the middle of the night by a strange humming sound coming from downstairs. All four friends found themselves drawn toward the library. They stood there dumbfounded as they heard beautiful music coming from The Storybook, which was opened to the map of The Crescendo River.

They looked at the map and exclaimed that they had never seen the colors look so vibrant, The Mountains of Tranquillity look so peaceful and the Sea of Adventure look so real with its shimmering, aquamarine waves. It all looked so real they would be sure and ask Great Aunt Nana who the wonderful artist was that had painted such a magnificent picture. Just as they were admiring a tall sailing ship on the emerald waves, Suzi started to actually get seasick from looking at the realistic picture. Then a wave of salt water splashed onto her cheek!

They realized that the beautiful music was coming from the center of the map, from the Box of Harmony and that what they were looking at was actually real, for now the picture had grown so big they were standing in the middle of the Land of Harmony!

The music was swirling all around them when what appeared to be a woman's face came toward them. They realized it was the faerie, Perfect Harmony! They were so excited, because they now realized that The Legend was actually not a legend after all, but the truth about the spirits of personalities.

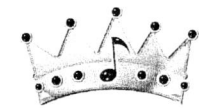

Chapter Eleven

More is revealed ...

The Scroll Marked XI

The very next thing, Wendy, Thomas, Suzi, and Sergio saw was The Royal Quartet! The four twins and the four friends met at the Center Bridge and shared a joy that was beyond description. Swing and Suzi fell into each other's arms. Waltz and Wendy were more subdued but greeted each other as long lost friends. Salsa and Sergio eyed each other with a wide smile and gave each other a big hug and a slap on the back. Tango and Thomas cautiously approached each other with a formal handshake, then realized that they shared such a personal bond they truly did feel like brothers, and finally embraced deeply.

Then Harmony the Faerie came toward them with a shimmering smile as she began to transform into a woman, a woman with a melodious voice, a voice, and face they recognized instantly as Briana Taylor—Great Aunt Nana!

"I'm sure you have figured out by now why I knew The Legend so well." She said. "But now that the message of **The Harmony Principle** has spread throughout the land, I am no longer needed here among your people. I long to return to my own home in The Land of Harmony." She then changed back to her natural youthful self of Harmony the Faerie.

What Harmony did next answered a question they had about the little wooden chest they had seen that first night they heard The Legend. She now took the ancient box and slipped off the leather straps, then she took out The Scroll Marked XI.

"My children, you have been so faithful to **The Harmony Principle**, spreading this most important message, that I have decided to give you the original scroll that was once entrusted to me. Practicing this principle was the main reason I accomplished so much success in your world. The other ten scrolls were success principles given to a worthy camel boy who later became the greatest salesman in the world." Then she flew off into the night sky of her own world.

Wendy, Thomas, Suzi, and Sergio stood there astonished. They would miss Great Aunt Nana, yet knew that because of her and **The Harmony Principle**, their lives, and the lives of countless others, were changed forever.

A New Life

One day, a few months later, the four friends were having a celebration lunch at The Café On The Rock, a bistro up in the forest near Cedar Springs River. The owners loved the scent of evergreens, the sounds of the rushing river, and songs of the mourning doves so much that they built the café around all of this. Small groups of tables were set up between boulders and trees. Some tables were even built right around the birch trees. Flowers weren't put in vases, but allowed to grow wild all over the ground.

Sergio was there with his shy teenage son, beaming with pride at his son's new job as a special needs counselor for kids. Wendy's husband praised his gracious wife in front of all her friends. This was a celebration luncheon giving thanks to all that had helped create the prosperity of their business.

Suzi was with her family, thanking them for their support and for putting up with her non-stop chatter for all these years! She was serene now, gladly letting others take center stage. The afternoon was complete when Thomas and his bride arrived together. Thomas wanted to thank his new wife with a toast, in front of the people that meant the most to him.

Why Can't Everyone Be Like Me?

"When I saw you at Celesta Pines something came alive in me," he began. "Your smile and sweet spirit touched my heart. Because of your unfailing faith in me and my imperfections I was able to realize my dream and be a part of Harmony 4. Thank you." The group let out a resounding, "Here, here!"

Just then a familiar musical sound came from within the evergreens. The four friends just smiled at each other and remembered the last thing Perfect Harmony had said to them: "Remember, dear ones, every time each of you sings your special harmony in life, spreading **The Harmony Principle** of tolerance and understanding, The Royal Quartet will come and greet you with a song of four-part harmony!"

The End—and now the beginning—of your personality journey!

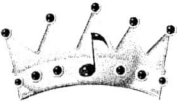

Save time and energy by accepting yourself and others as they are!

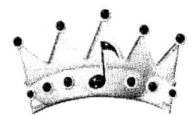

Your Personality Kingdom™
Like four part harmony, each personality is needed.

Part Four

Author's Note

Reference Charts

Personality Kingdoms At-a-glance

Quick Personality Test

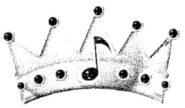

AUTHOR'S NOTE

Through this brief introduction you have received a glimpse into understanding a very important concept that will affect you in all areas of your life: work, relationships, school and more.

You learned that we can categorize people, not to label them, but to help understand them. You learned that if we ask ourselves certain questions, we can easily identify ourselves and others. Just like in the story, you can determine your personality style by seeing where you live on The Crescendo River of Energy. You can accomplish this by asking two easy questions:

"What Royal Family do I belong to—the Family of Introvert or Extrovert?"

"What side of the river do I usually live on—the Feeling or Thinking side?"

Even though you may be from one predominate Personality Kingdom, or a combination, your Personality Kingdom will have its own special sound. Just as different singers may sing a song, it is still clearly recognizable as the same tune.

You will begin to look at people in a new light. In fact, most people that understand this concept begin to see different personalities fairly easily. Depending on *your* personality style, you may be tempted to walk right up to someone and blurt out "Oh, hi! You're from the Tango Kingdom, just look at you! Your hair is perfect, and you are so precise. It's obvious." I use this example, because I was there when my Swing friend walked right up to a complete stranger and said those exact words to him!

Important: don't tell people what you think they are, just keep your conclusions to yourself. Also be careful not to draw those conclusions in haste, remember we don't always act the same. Just say that you know of a fun book about personalities and tolerance that they might want to read.

Like many people who have heard of Your Personality Kingdom, you may find yourself very excited about this fun and valuable tool. An excellent way to internalize a new concept is to share it with someone else. It has also been shown that when you involve as many senses as possible, you will remember and retain the information longer. Therefore, I encourage you to use *Your Personality Kingdom's* videos and audiotapes/CD's. You will be able to see and hear what your Personality Kingdom looks like and sounds like!

I hope you came to appreciate the special person you are and that no ONE Personality Kingdom is better than another is. Remember to let your special music blend in with others. Sing your unique part in life, because we need each other to make the world complete.

Thank you for letting me share these insights with you, and happy dancing through life in perfect harmony!

On a sunny day in May…

Kimberly M'Lady West

Celesta Pines Cottage, Mason City, Iowa

Quick Personality Test – Part One
Extrovert or Introvert

In just two steps, this easy test will determine what your <u>predominate</u> personality style is. First, determine if you are mostly an Extrovert or Introvert. The question is not, "DO I have this trait?" But, rather, "What is MORE like me?" When choosing between the two personality traits, ask yourself this question:

Example: "Am I *more* Shy, <u>or</u> Outgoing?" Choose just one word, and try not to skip words.

We all act differently in certain situations, so place your answer next to the word that describes you MOST of the time. There are no "best" answers, so be honest, and have fun! Not sure? Ask a close friend or relative how they see you.

Most of the time am I more…

b. ___ Loud	or	a. ___ Quiet	
b. ___ Outgoing at parties	or	a. ___ Shy at parties	
a. ___ Low-energy	or	b. ___ High-energy	
b. ___ Direct	or	a. ___ Indirect	
a. ___ Set in ways	or	b. ___ Adventurous	
a. ___ Peaceful	or	b. ___ Restless	
b. ___ Risk-taker	or	a. ___ Cautious	
a. ___ Passive	or	b. ___ Assertive	
a. ___ Reserved	or	b. ___ Outspoken	
b. ___ Energy filled from others	or	a. ___ Energy filled from within	

Scoring-Choose One

1 = Yes, that's me.

2 = Really me.

3 = <u>Very</u> much me.

Under stress am I more…

a. ___ Withdrawn	or	b. ___ Can't relax
a. ___ Insecure	or	b. ___ Impatient
b. ___ Interrupting	or	a. ___ Silent
b. ___ Dominate	or	a. ___ Depressed
a. ___ Stubborn	or	b. ___ Intense-dramatic

Simply add up all scores for each letter. To eliminate errors, cross off your answers as you score. Double-check your scores.

Total: **"a"** _____ for **Introvert.**   **"b"** _____ for **Extrovert.** (15-45 points)

Personality Test – Part Two

Feeling or Thinking Approach to Life

Now, that you have determined if you are an Extrovert or Introvert, let's determine your approach to life—Feeling or Thinking.

Most of the time am I more…

a. ___ Flexible	or	b. ___ Planned		
a. ___ Late	or	b. ___ On-time		
b. ___ Fact oriented	or	a. ___ Dream oriented		
b. ___ Reserved	or	a. ___ Personable		
a. ___ Emotional	or	b. ___ Private		
b. ___ Formal with people	or	a. ___ Informal with people		
a. ___ Relationship focused	or	b. ___ Results focused		
a. ___ Scattered in thought	or	b. ___ Linear in thought		
b. ___ Independent in work	or	a. ___ Group oriented		
a. ___ Relaxed	or	b. ___ Needing to accomplish things		
b. ___ Polite	or	a. ___ Warm and friendly		

Scoring-Choose One

1 = Yes, that's me.

2 = Really me.

3 = <u>Very</u> much me.

Under stress am I more…

a. ___ Indecisive or b. ___ Demanding
b. ___ Obsessive-compulsive or a. ___ Absent-minded
b. ___ Rigid or a. ___ Disorganized
a. ___ Lazy or b. ___ Controlling

Simply add up all scores for each letter. To eliminate errors, cross off your answers as you score. Double-check your scores.

Total score: "a" _____ for **Feeling.** "b" score _____ for **Thinking.** (15-45 points)

_____ **Introvert or Extrovert** (from part one)

_____ **Feeling or Thinking** (from part two)

Now let's put them together. Circle Your Personality Kingdom!

Introvert-Feeling = Waltz Kingdom

Introvert-Thinking = Tango Kingdom

Extrovert-Feeling = Swing Kingdom

Extrovert-Thinking = Salsa Kingdom

Note: If you scored evenly, you need to complete each pair of phrases. (Meaning you skipped some.) If your scores are very close, you may be a combination of personality styles.

Continue reading the following pages to find out your strengths and possible weaknesses. Or read the entire book to have a complete picture of Your Personality Kingdom.

Your Personality Kingdom
Like four part harmony, each personality is needed.

©2003 Kimberly West from the book *Why Can't Everyone Be Like Me?*

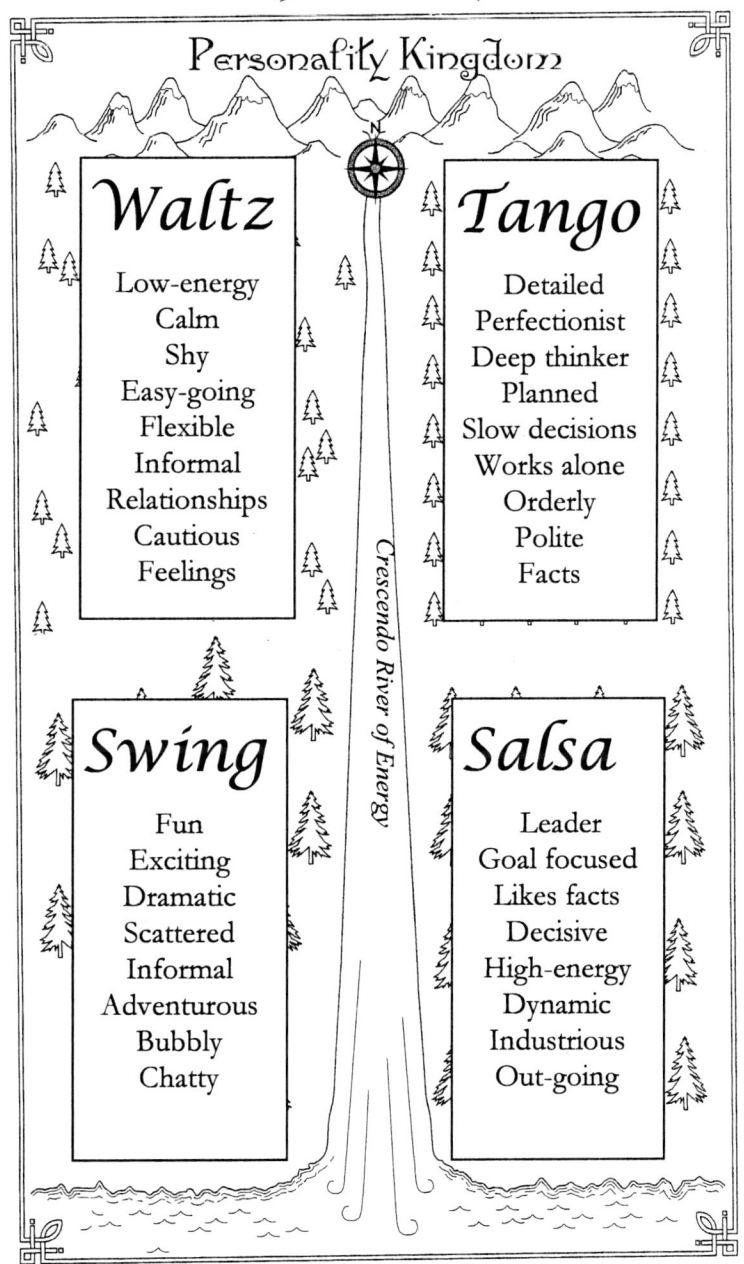

The Royal Quartet

Waltz the Warm-Hearted	Tango the Thinker
Swing the Star	Salsa the Supreme

"Like four-part harmony, each personality kingdom is needed."

Family of Introvert

Waltz the Warm-Hearted

Royal Cottage

"Relax—Have A Nice Day"

Why Can't Everyone Be Like Me?

CHARACTER STRENGTHS -- THE KINGDOM OF WALTZ THE WARM-HEARTED

Accommodating	Adaptable
Agreeable	Considerate
Amiable	Contented
Cautious	Counseling skills
Compassionate	Easy-going
Diplomatic	Good administrator
Gracious	Informal
Humble	Likable
Loyal friend	Patient
Mediator	Prefers first names
Modest	Respectful
Relaxed	Rise to the occasion
Reserved	Shy
Supportive	Steady and calm
Team-player	Tolerant
Sympathetic	Warm & Friendly

WALTZ THE WARM-HEARTED—POSSIBLE CHARACTER WEAKNESSES

Acquiesce (give in)	Absent-minded
Avoids responsibility	Apathetic
Bashful	Cluttered
Depressed	Disorganized
Doubtful	Fearful
Late	Indecisive
Martyr	Lazy
Others more important	Passive
Passive/aggressive	Quiet will of steel
Poor self-esteem	Self-righteous
Says yes, means no	Stubborn
Slow	Stuck in rut
Sluggish	Two-faced
Unenthusiastic	Unmotivated
Worrier	Wishy-washy

Family of Introvert

Tango the Thinker

Royal Inventor's Palace

"Have Order—Strive for Perfection"

Why Can't Everyone Be Like Me?

CHARACTER STRENGTHS—THE KINGDOM OF TANGO THE THINKER

Analytical	Conservative
Cautious	Courteous
Deep emotions	Deep thinker
Detailed	Follows the rules
Dry humor	Frugal, thrifty
Duty, honor bound	Intellectual
Genius prone	Low-energy
Gifted	Neat, organized
High-standards	Patient
Likes charts, graphs	Persistent
Methodical	Private
Planner	Problem-solver
Respectful	Proper
Scheduled	Responsible
Serious	Slow and steady
Structured	Works well alone

TANGO THE THINKER -- POSSIBLE CHARACTER WEAKNESSES

Bogged down in planning	Caught up in details
Can't say, "I'm wrong"	Critical
Cheap, too frugal	Demands perfection
Hard on self	False humility
Hyper sensitive	Fussy, picky
Hypochondriac	Hard to get moving
Insecure	Not a team player
Isolated	Obsessive-compulsive
Low self-image	Pessimistic
Perfectionist	Poor social skills
Resentful	Self-righteous
Sets impossible standards	Slow to act
Takes things personally	Stubborn
Tends toward depression	Too emotional
Unforgiving	Withdrawn

Family of Extrovert

Swing the Star

Royal Tree House

"Have Fun!"

Why Can't Everyone Be Like Me?

CHARACTER STRENGTHS -- THE KINGDOM OF SWING THE STAR

Animated	Cute
Bubbly	Delightful
Charming	Dramatic
Entertainer	Enthusiastic
Fast-paced	Exciting
Great socializer	Flexible
Happy	Friendly
Involved	Fun-loving
Lively	Funny
Loves action	Intuitive
Playful	Light-hearted
Relationship focused	Optimistic
Risk-taker	Outgoing
Spontaneous	Persuasive
Stimulating	Popular
Talkative	Sparkling

Why Can't Everyone Be Like Me?

SWING THE STAR -- POSSIBLE CHARACTER WEAKNESSES

Angered easily	Childish
Answers for others	Doesn't finish projects
Cluttered	Easily distracted
Disorganized	Egotistical
Dominates conversations	Fickle, unstable
Exaggerates stories	Impulsive
Forgetful	Interrupts
Hates to be alone	Invasive of other's space
Hyper, restless energy	Losses things
Loud voice and laugh	Not time oriented
Poor follow-through	Scatterbrained
Shallow	Seems insincere
Show-off	Talks too much
Superficial	Too dramatic
Unproductive	Undisciplined

Family of Extrovert

Salsa the Supreme

Royal Castle

"Achieve Great Things—Do It Now!"

Why Can't Everyone Be Like Me?

CHARACTER STRENGTHS -- THE KINGDOM OF SALSA THE SUPREME

Accomplished	Ambitious
Adventurous	Brave
Assumes authority	Causes action
Capable	Daring
Commands attention	Delegates tasks
Confident	Doer
Decisive	Fast-paced
Direct	Independent
Dominate	Leader
Industrious	Outspoken
Productive	Persuasive
Resourceful	Powerful
Results oriented	Practical
Take-charge	Problem solver
Tenacious	Risk-taker
Visionary	Strong-willed

Why Can't Everyone Be Like Me?

SALSA THE SUPREME -- POSSIBLE CHARACTER WEAKNESSES

Aggressive	Bursts of rage
Argumentative	Cold-unemotional
Arrogant	Comes on too strong
Blunt	Controlling
Bossy	Crafty, manipulative
Can do everything better	Cruel
Can't relax	Domineering
Can't say, "I'm sorry"	End justifies the means
Decides for others	Impatient
Demanding	Inflexible, rigid
Know-it-all attitude	Interrupts
Negative, sarcastic	Not sensitive to others
Short-tempered	Rude
Stubborn	Tactless
Unaffectionate	Workaholic

Shared Personality Traits
Introvert or Extrovert Family

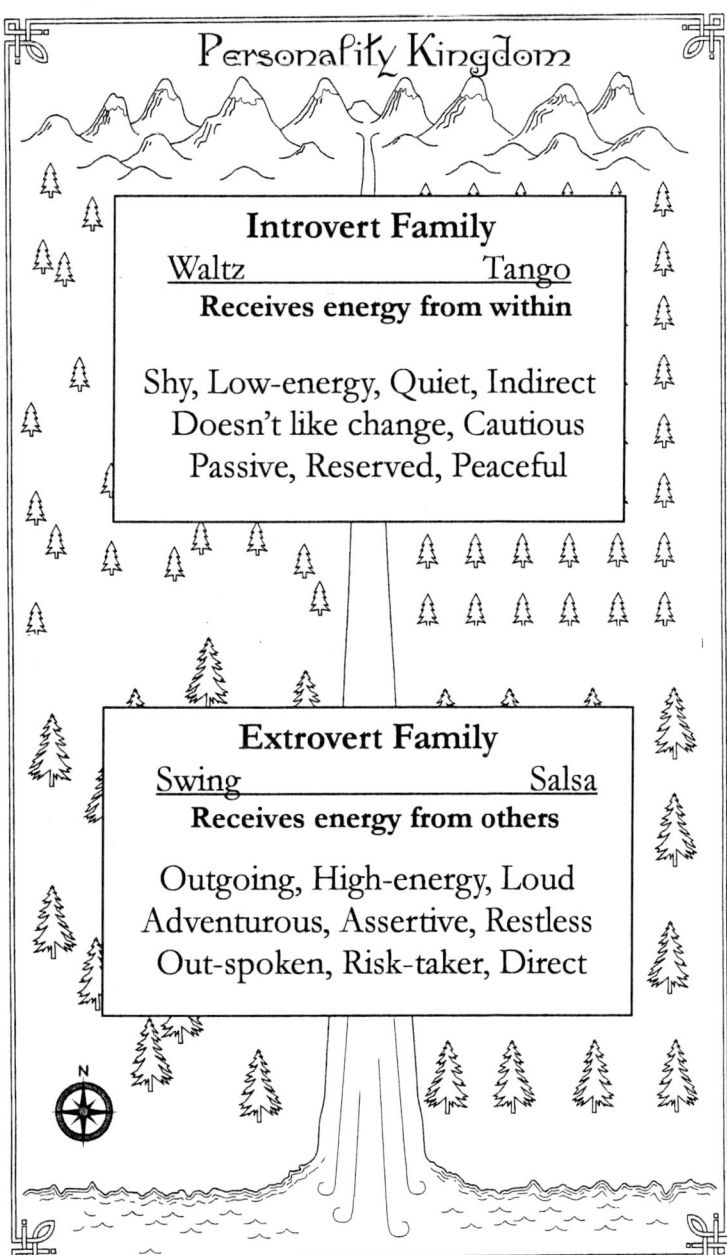

Personality Kingdom

Introvert Family

Waltz   Tango

Receives energy from within

Shy, Low-energy, Quiet, Indirect
Doesn't like change, Cautious
Passive, Reserved, Peaceful

Extrovert Family

Swing   Salsa

Receives energy from others

Outgoing, High-energy, Loud
Adventurous, Assertive, Restless
Out-spoken, Risk-taker, Direct

Shared Personality Traits
Feeling or Thinking Outlook

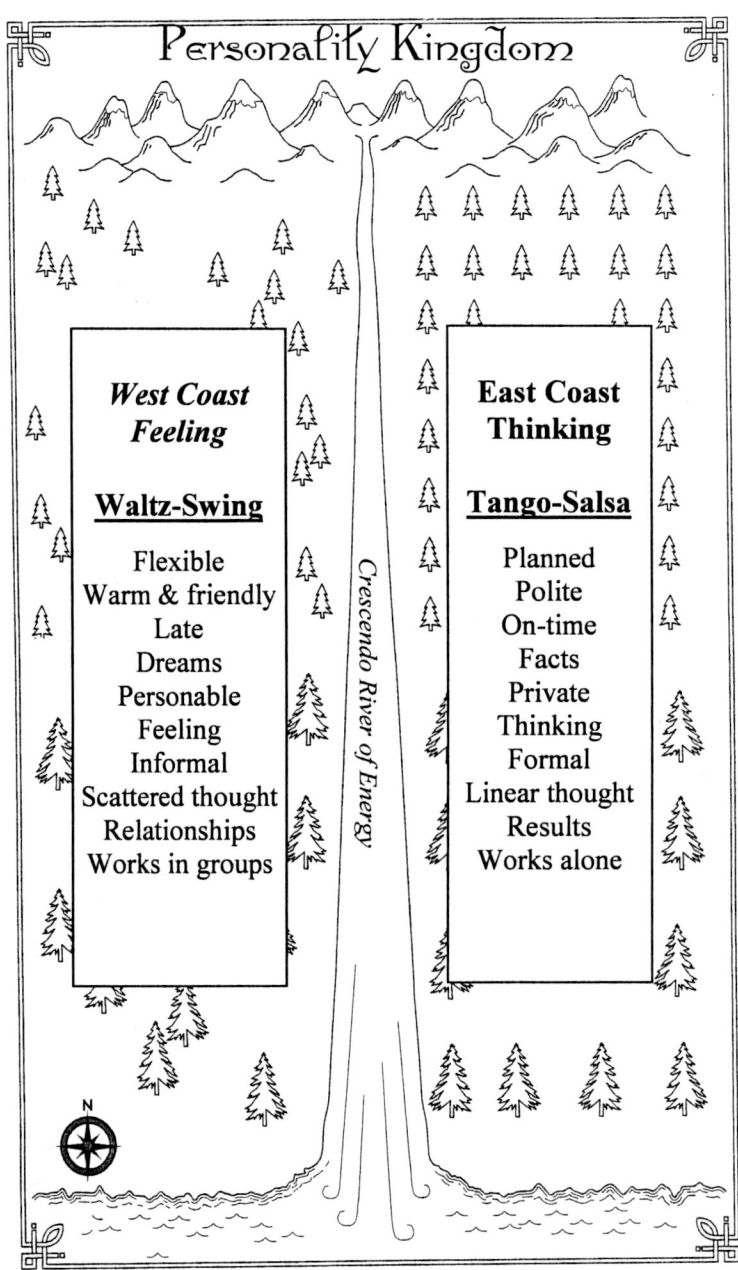

♪ **Words that are "Music To My Ears"** ♪
Say them to gain instant rapport with each style

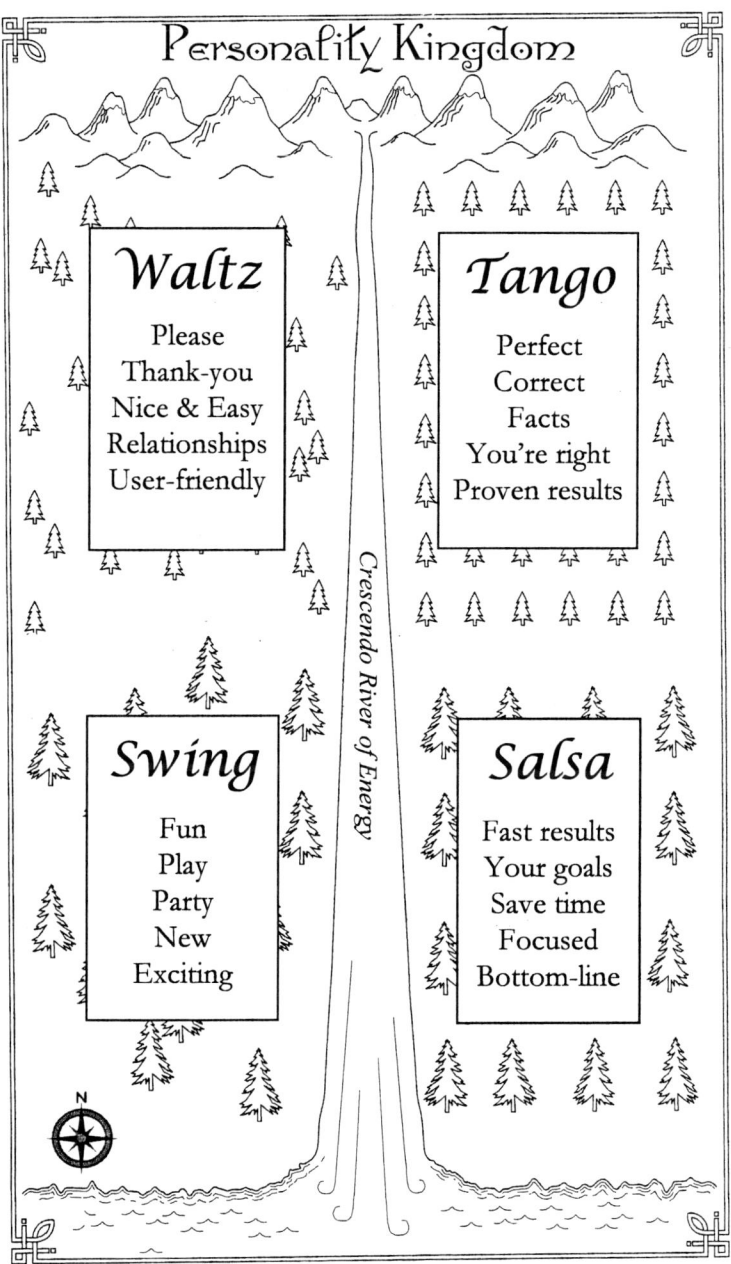

EASY WAYS TO IDENTIFY PERSONALITY KINGDOM

	Introvert Family		Extrovert Family	
	Waltz	**Tango**	**Swing**	**Salsa**
Clothes	Comfy	Perfect	Bright	Practical
Shoes	Comfy	Conservative	Fashionable	Sturdy
Voice	Quiet	Articulate	Loud	Strong
Gestures	Easygoing	Close to body	Expansive	Powerful
Work area	Cluttered	Neat, few projects	Neat, many projects	Messy
Emotional Need	Peace	To be right	Attention	Control
Walk	Slow	Careful	Bouncy	Fast
Energy	Low	Low	High	High
Time-frame	Past	Past	Future	Now!
Humor	Witty	Dry	Raucous	Sarcastic
Outlook	Positive	Pessimistic	Optimistic	Negative
Conversation	Listener	Precise	Chatty	Bottom-line
Social Needs	Appreciated	Valued for quality	Praise	Recognition
Change	Dislikes	Dislikes	Loves	Likes

DECISIONS * CONFLICT * PROBLEM-SOLVING

	Introvert Family		Extrovert Family	
	Waltz	**Tango**	**Swing**	**Salsa**
Conflict	♦ Abhors ♦ Avoids at all costs ♦ Will tell you what you want to hear, but do what they want.	♦ Doesn't like ♦ Will face with determination to do the job right.	♦ Avoids ♦ Doesn't like ♦ Makes jokes about it	♦ Faces directly ♦ Decisive ♦ Appears fearless
Decision Making	♦ Slowly ♦ Based on feelings ♦ Everybody happy with it ♦ Likes others to decide at times	♦ Very slowly ♦ Gathers all data ♦ Based on how it was done in the past ♦ Results focused	♦ Impulsively ♦ Based on how it feels ♦ Others approval ♦ Fashionable	♦ Fast ♦ Impatient ♦ Based on facts ♦ Goal-oriented
Problem-Solving	♦ Waits, avoids ♦ Hopes will just go away ♦ Lets other handle	♦ Slow ♦ Formulate plan ♦ Looks at all options, data ♦ Looks at how it was done in the past.	♦ Waits until last minute ♦ Chaotic ♦ Gets others to help ♦ Charming	♦ Very fast ♦ Delegates ♦ Gathers facts ♦ Confident

Personality Styles Comparison Chart

The Royal Quartet West	Waltz	Tango	Swing	Salsa
	Your Personality Kingdom			
Hippocrates & Littauer	Phlegmatic	Melancholy	Choleric	Sanguine
Merrill-Reid Soc. Styles	Amiable	Analytical	Driver	Expressive
DISC System	S Supportive	C Compliance	I Influence	D Dominance
Alessandra	Relater	Thinker	Socializer	Director
Myers-Briggs*	INF	INT	ESP	ESJ

Note: This chart is based on my opinion of the systems that I am familiar with.
* Some of the categories do not fit neatly into one personality style. I include it here because of the popularity of the system.

Postscript – Contact Us

Congratulations! You are one of the first readers to experience this innovative and fun concept. Have you enjoyed reading this book? We would love to hear from you to receive your valuable feedback. Because this is such a revolutionary concept, we decided to release a pre-publication manual edition first. The final version will be a standard 5 ½ x 8 ½ hardback edition, with updated graphics. Let us know what you liked about the book, any suggestions you may have, and what impact it has had on your life.

What type of follow-up book would you like to see next—Teens? Children's picture book? Business? Relationships? Parenting? As you can imagine the possibilities of more fun stories with The Royal Quartet are endless!

Do you have a story that exemplifies a certain Personality Kingdom? Maybe an amusing anecdote that perfectly highlights a certain personality? Or do you have a Harmony Principle success story that you would like to share? Please contact us, it really does make my day to hear from you. The sincere desire to make a difference in people's lives is the reason I wrote this book.

Feel free to visit my Web site or contact me at the address below for information on speaking or training opportunities for your organization. We will gladly forward a complete media packet upon request.

We know that your life is busy. If you include your address, phone, e-mail or fax number we will be happy to answer your correspondence.

Need a speaker? Looking for a truly unique experience?

Kimberly West is the only person to use music, storytelling and live costumed dance couples as visual aids in her presentations on personality styles. It's dynamic, fun, entertaining and life changing!

Kimberly West
Your Personality Kingdom™
Box 512, Mason City, IA 50402-0512

tele. 641.423.2123 ♪ www.harmony4.net ♪ fax 641.423.1404

e-mail: FunSpeaker@msn.com

or Harmony4you@hotmail.com

Order Form

Your Personality Kingdom™
Like four part harmony, each personality is needed.

Order Form – Page 1 of 2

"Why Can't Everyone Be Like Me?"

ISBN #		$ Qty.
0-9742514-1-0	Hardback Edition 5½ x 8½ 190 pages	$19.95____
0-9742514-0-2	Manual Edition 8½ x 11 (Paperback) 172 pages (Same content with room for notes.)	$17.95____
0-9742514-2-9	♪ Book-on-tape – Unabridged version 6 Cassettes with music for each Personality Kingdom	$29.95____

<u>Read by the author in a lively, animated, and soothing voice.</u>

0-9742514-3-7	♪ Book-on-tape – Abridged version with music 2 Cassettes *The Legend* only (part two from the book)	$19.95____

VIDEO #001 ♪ Video – VHS Introduction to the 4 Personality $19.95____
   Kingdoms. Live seminar with dancers, skits, music. Color 66 minutes. Hear and see what your Personality Kingdom looks and sounds like!

AUDIO #001 ♪ 90 Minute Live seminar-on-tape. 2 Tape Series $19.95____
   Intro to 4 styles, careers, stress, group activity, music (different content from video)

✱KIT #101   ♪ Full success kit—includes hardback book, $77.00____
   full book-on-tape, audio seminar, and video.   Save 15% BEST VALUE

Name _____

Address _____

_____

Telephone number #_____

e-mail:_____Signature_____

_____   _____
Master Card or Visa #   Exp. Date

Call for quantity or corporate discounts. Gift service available—we ship to your list!

> **Go to next page for order summary & shipping charges**

(PAGE 2 OF 2) ORDER SUMMARY FOR: _____ (NAME)

ISBN	DESC.	PRICE	QUANTITY	= TOTAL
0-9742514-0-3	HARDBACK	$19.95		$
0-9742514-0-2	MANUAL EDITION	$17.95		$
0-9742514-0-4	UNABRIDGED BOOK ON TAPE	$29.95		$
0-9742514-0-5	ABRIDGED BOOK ON TAPE	$19.95		$
VIDEO #001	VHS-VIDEO	$19.95		$
AUDIO #002	LIVE SEMINAR ON TAPE	$19.95		$
KIT #101	BOOK, TAPES, VIDEO	$77.00		$
			TOTAL ITEMS	$
		IOWA RESIDENTS	ADD 6.5% SALES TAX	$
			PRIORITY SHIPPING & HANDLING	$ 4.00 (PER ORDER)
			GRAND TOTAL DUE	$

TO ORDER:

Fax Both Pages to: (641) 423-1404 or **Call:** (641) 423-2123 or
Mail to: Your Personality Kingdom, Box 512, Mason City, IA 50402-0512

Enclose check or money order

Order Form – Page 1 of 2

"Why Can't Everyone Be Like Me?"

ISBN #		$ Qty.

ISBN #	Description	Price
0-9742514-1-0	Hardback Edition 5½ x 8½ 190 pages	$19.95____
0-9742514-0-2	Manual Edition 8½ x 11 (Paperback) 172 pages (Same content with room for notes.)	$17.95____
0-9742514-2-9	♪ Book-on-tape – Unabridged version 6 Cassettes with music for each Personality Kingdom	$29.95____

<u>Read by the author in a lively, animated, and soothing voice.</u>

0-9742514-3-7	♪ Book-on-tape – Abridged version with music 2 Cassettes *The Legend* only (part two from the book)	$19.95____

VIDEO #001 ♪ Video – VHS Introduction to the 4 Personality $19.95____
Kingdoms. Live seminar with dancers, skits, music. Color 66 minutes. Hear and see what your Personality Kingdom looks and sounds like!

AUDIO #001 ♪ 90 Minute Live seminar-on-tape. 2 Tape Series $19.95____
Intro to 4 styles, careers, stress, group activity, music (different content from video)

*KIT #101   ♪ Full success kit—includes hardback book, $77.00____
full book-on-tape, audio seminar, and video.   Save 15% BEST VALUE

Name _____

Address _____

_____

Telephone number #_____

e-mail:_____Signature_____

_____ _____
Master Card or Visa #   Exp. Date

Call for quantity or corporate discounts. Gift service available—we ship to your list!

> **Go to next page for order summary & shipping charges**

(PAGE 2 OF 2) ORDER SUMMARY FOR: _____ (NAME)

ISBN	DESC.	PRICE	QUANTITY	= TOTAL
0-9742514-0-3	HARDBACK	$19.95		$
0-9742514-0-2	MANUAL EDITION	$17.95		$
0-9742514-0-4	UNABRIDGED BOOK ON TAPE	$29.95		$
0-9742514-0-5	ABRIDGED BOOK ON TAPE	$19.95		$
VIDEO #001	VHS-VIDEO	$19.95		$
AUDIO #002	LIVE SEMINAR ON TAPE	$19.95		$
KIT #101	BOOK, TAPES, VIDEO	$77.00		$
			TOTAL ITEMS	$
		IOWA RESIDENTS	ADD 6.5% SALES TAX	$
			PRIORITY SHIPPING & HANDLING	$ 4.00 (PER ORDER)
			GRAND TOTAL DUE	$

TO ORDER:

Fax Both Pages to: **(641) 423-1404** or **Call**: **(641) 423-2123** or
Mail to: Your Personality Kingdom, Box 512, Mason City, IA 50402-0512

Enclose check or money order

About the Author

Kimberly West, founder of Your Personality Kingdom, has given workshops, training programs and keynote speeches to a wide variety of organizations. From corporate business sessions to women's church groups, Kimberly delights her audience with a truly entertaining and valuable program. She is the only person to use music, storytelling, and live costumed dance couples as visual aids in her personality presentations. The audience members get to see and hear what their personality style looks like and sounds like. She is also a member of the Iowa National Speakers Association, The National Wellness Institute, and USA Ballroom Dancers Association.

Kimberly is a former teacher, counselor, and business executive. She started out detassling corn in Iowa, then was employed by the local mayor and quickly worked her way up the corporate ladder. At twenty-three, she became the only woman and youngest person to hold a corporate financial executive position for a Fortune 500 company. She went on in similar positions for Architectural Digest and Pactel Cellular companies. Because of this accomplishment, she was included in Who's Who in The West.

Kimberly is also an involved person. While living in Pasadena, California, she was a member of The Tournament of Roses Association, where she loved interacting with people from all over the world.

She was born on a military base in Anchorage, Alaska, and moved when she was just three months old. This was a prophetic start, as she eventually relocated fifty-one times in her life! Now, Kimberly recently migrated back to her beloved home state of Iowa. She is glad to be there with her family that is mostly from Swing's Tree House. When she is not traveling for speaking engagements, you can find her in Iowa, either writing her next book, or laughing with her fun family!

FOUR KEYS TO THE HARMONY PRINCIPLE

KEY #1

LIKE A SONG OF FOUR-PART HARMONY,
EACH PERSONALITY KINGDOM IS NEEDED.

KEY #2

TREASURE YOUR PERSONALITY KINGDOM–
KNOW HOW YOU DANCE THROUGH LIFE.

KEY #3

KNOW HOW YOUR ACTIONS AFFECT OTHERS.

KEY #4

ADJUST YOUR ACTIONS TO BE IN TUNE WITH OTHERS.
TREAT PEOPLE THE WAY <u>THEY</u> WANT TO BE TREATED.

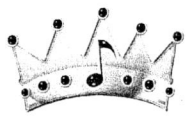

Your Personality Kingdom™
Like four part harmony, each personality is needed.

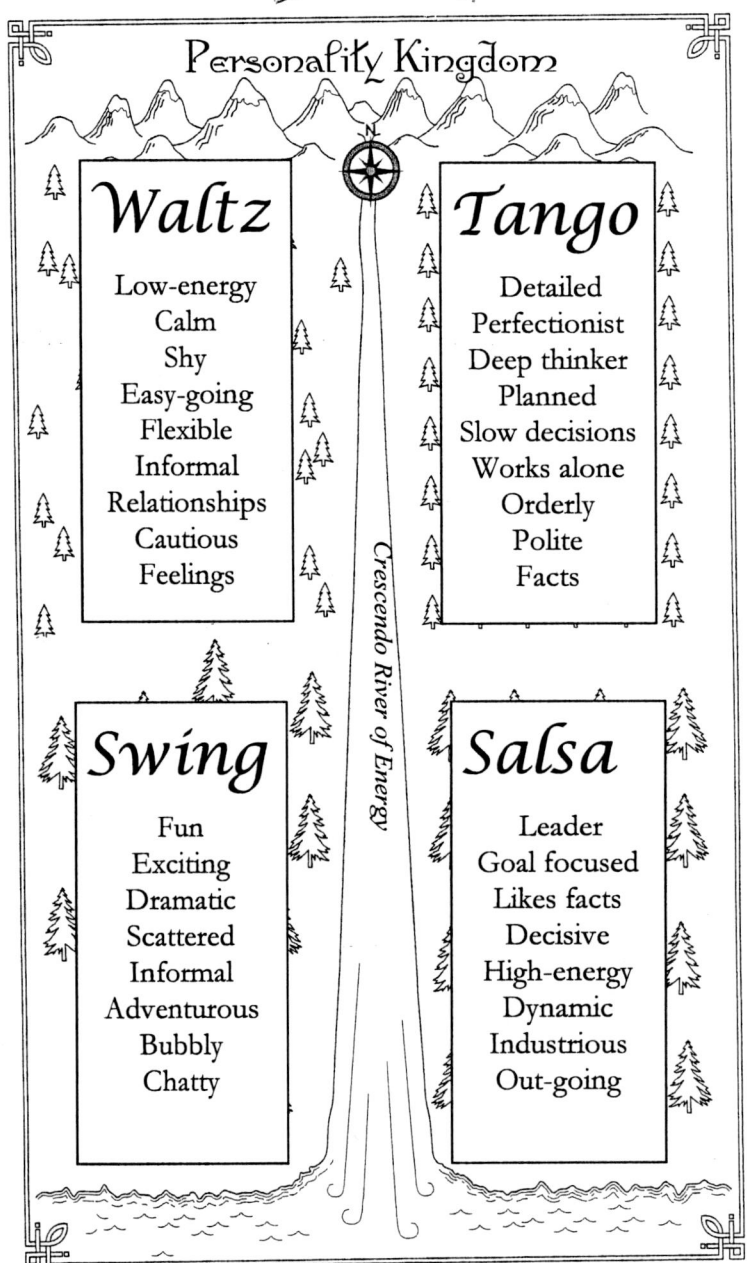